**Community Care
Practice Handbooks**

General Editor: Martin Davies

Children In and Out of Care

Alan Ishaq

10/91

Community Care Practice Handbooks

General Editor: Martin Davies

Children In and Out of Care

Claire Wendelken

First published in 1983 by Heinemann Educational Books Ltd
Reprinted in 1987 by
Wildwood House Limited
Gower House
Croft Road
Aldershot
Hants GU11 3HR
England

Distributed by
Gower Publishing Company
Old Post Road
Brookfield
Vermont 05036
USA

British Library Cataloguing in Publication Data
Wendelken, Claire
   Children in and out of care - (Community care
   practice handbooks; 13)
   1. Children - Care and hygiene
   2. Child welfare - Great Britain
   I. Title   II. Series
   362.7'0941   HQ777.6

ISBN 0 7045 0587 8

Phototypesetting by Georgia Origination, Liverpool
Printed and bound in Great Britain by
Biddles Ltd, Guildford and King's Lynn

Contents

Acknowledgements

Like so many authors I owe a deep gratitude to many colleagues, students and friends who encouraged me, tried out the exercises and criticised the drafts. In particular I wish to thank Susan McCaskie, my colleague in social services, for her detailed comments and discussions with me; Jenny Kendrick, specialist worker with under 5s, for her early reading and comments on Chapter 3; Sue Allen and Gill Munrow for their original list of feelings of those involved in a reception into care, incorporated in Chapter 4; Cheryl Tidmarsh for her help while a training officer in social services, in working out the basis for the placement exercise in Chapter 5, and Madeleine Kinlon, training officer and colleague at Bedford College, for letting me try out so many of the ideas on her. I am indebted to Ian Vallender of the National Children's Bureau Library who has been endlessly helpful and patient concerning all my inquiries. I am grateful to Sue Paxton, who has typed and retyped the manuscript, her enthusiasm for the project enabling its completion.

Above all, however, my thanks go to my husband, Alan, whose love, patience, support and encouragement have made it possible for me to write this book.

Introduction

For anyone starting in social work with children and families the
problem is often where to begin, while for those with experience it
may be difficult to obtain fresh ideas. Social work training may
give you particular skills in methods and help you develop a
personal style and thorough knowledge of yourself. None the less,
for the trained and untrained alike, there remain large areas of
'how do I do it' and 'what do I need to know in order to do it well'
that have to be discovered in relation to your own agency.

Working with children is costly; clear decisions about what to do
and how best to do it can save both time and emotional wear and
tear, so I have aimed to give guidelines and check-lists to clarify
your tasks. None of us ever quite manages to grasp *all* the essential
points. I have tried to give you enough detail to stretch your
perspective and challenge you, without drowning you in irrel-
evancies.

For experienced staff I hope some of the ideas may cause you to
examine your own current practice. I know my own constantly
needs renewing and improving. The ideas are not to be taken as
'doing it by the book' but as suggestions that a supervisor might
offer to help you plan your work. Many of them originate from
supervision of staff and students who tried them out and found
them useful.

The legal framework for child care is complex. I have referred
to particular sections of the legislation where it forms an integral
part of the social work practice but this is not a detailed legal
handbook. Intermediate Treatment, child abuse, fostering and
adoption are all referred to, but the specialist information and tech-
niques in these fields require their own separate practice manuals.
There is already a wealth of literature specific to them. The task of
preventive work is also a complex one, involving a variety of skills
and often reflecting local resources. I have outlined a way in which
a family's needs may be identified, but not attempted to cover
treatment plans owing to problems of space. This volume is for the
generic beginner.

Each chapter contains lists of 'tools' for the worker to get
together to improve her practice. For simplicity I have used the
feminine gender when referring to the social worker and the
masculine when referring to the child. Where possible I have used

parent rather than mother as the term for the person at home caring for the child. What I say is set against a local authority frame of reference, but some of the ideas have originated from, and may be of interest to, the voluntary child care societies, who continue to act as pioneers in so many spheres.

The exercises suggested are suitable for a small group to do with their supervisor, or to use on training courses. No answers are supplied as the 'right' solution will vary according to local policy and resources. The aim is to provide material that will stimulate but not constrain, so that the group focuses on the issue involved rather than on the intimate detail of an individual's real case history.

The ethical stance I hold is that it is highly desirable for a child to participate in decision-making about his own life, as expounded by Voice of the child in care,* and legally strengthened by the Child Care Act 1980, Section 18(1). However, I am also firmly convinced that children need emotional security and boundaries to their powerfulness, in order to grow and develop. This may involve taking decisions about them. We need reminders and stimulation to keep the child's welfare central to our work, but above all every child should have adults who show love and commitment to him and his future, and who do not disappear as the child begins to trust them.

The following is one practitioner's viewpoint, influenced by many colleaues and students, to be challenged and changed by you, as you try out the ideas and suggestions offered here.

---

* A registered charity concerned to encourage a child-centred service for children in care. Secretary: Gwen James, 60 Carysfort Rd, London N8.

1 Basic Equipment for Assessment

In this chapter I am seeking to highlight the problems assessments pose and the basic information that you should have before you meet a family. I am not looking at the various methods of casework, family therapy or behaviour modification and their different approaches to assessing family relationships.

The role your supervisor plays will be crucial in clarifying your task. You will need to take back to her a range of information for discussion, and to submit your judgements, opinions and conclusions to a detailed scrutiny. With her, departmental policy will be explicitly brought to bear on the family's or child's needs.

I have gathered together the six main considerations you and your supervisor will need to look at, under the headings Purpose, Pain, Policy, Posterity, Place and People. Under each I have listed some of the questions to which you should seek answers in your own authority. These will influence the decisions you will take as the social worker responsible for an individual case, and the decisions of the families you aim to help.

The lists are to trigger ideas and help you focus what you want to know. They are far from comprehensive and you should expect to add your own dimension to them.

Purpose

The generic name of assessment is used to cover a wide range of purpose and you may be asked to undertake 'an assessment' in work with families and children: (a) for day care; (b) because of concern about a child's development or home situation; (c) because the child needs to be received into care, or (d) is before the juvenile court which has requested reports on his home situation.

The different purposes for which you do assessment work should be reflected in the level of information gathering and sharing that you undertake. However, in every assessment situation there remains the possibility that your involvement will reveal wider issues and deeper problems. The family's request for help beyond the original purpose for your involvement needs to be viewed against the problems of resource allocation and the suitability of your agency for the task. A change in role as a result of what you discover should always be made explicit to the family concerned. For example, if you approach a family as a result of a court appearance, and the court gives no direction for your futher involvement, then you must be clear with the family that it is not with the authority of the court that you are offering to help with problems in family relationships.

Questions about purpose

For whom am I undertaking this work? The child? The parents? The court?

What information is relevant to that purpose?

What more do I need to know to assess the truth of the initial information given?

Do I have the right to go beyond that initial purpose if invited to do so? If I recognise other needs?

Pain

Assesment is to do with measuring and, sometimes, concluding that something is not good enough. It includes recognising strengths (an aspect that is often omitted, particulary in reports to courts), not avoiding conflicts, and confronting people with issues that they would rather ignore. It may be that the family is not caring enough, that the child is not developing as he should, that the community has not got the right resources to meet the needs of this family, or that the court decides that the child is not conforming enough. Each of these 'nots' contains the pain of child or family, the judgement of someone and, implicitly, a need for change.

For many families the involvement of a social worker is an intrusion on their privacy, conflicting with their cultural mores. Acceptance of help from what is perceived as authority may cause shame, confusion or pain. In carrying out your task as a social worker, do not allow yourself to lose sight of whose pain you are causing or alleviating, whose judgement you are reinforcing, and whether the change being brought about could be effected less painfully.

The pain you experience when you discover that the community or your authority has not got the resources to meet the needs of a particular child should not be ignored. It can be channelled into recording on the child's file what you consider would have been appropriate to the need at that stage, collecting material to show that other children have the same needs and challenging your Director of Social Services regarding policy. You may also be able to explore the possibility of a voluntary society developing that kind of resource in your area.

The separation of parents and children, whether by request, or decision of the court, incorporates loss and fear for all concerned. Your own pain at this time can rush you into false reassurances to mask the true situation. Assessment work requires the professional discipline of allowing your client's pain to be fully acknowledged and yet not avoiding painful conclusions nor resulting action.

Questions about pain
What support is there for acknowledging pain in decision-making?
– With the family? with the child?
Do colleagues share painful decisions, or are they left to you alone?
Does 'colleague' only apply to field social workers, or does it apply across professional disciplines?
Is supervision merely case management, or is it also a place where personal costs are discussed?

Policy
Policy is often regarded by social workers as remote edicts from on high. In brighter authorities and as a growing practice to bridge this gap, social workers are being invited into planning groups to share their perspective of problems. When you start in an authority, you need time to learn how the legislation is interpreted and used, and how your own department is linked with housing, education and health services. The kinds and quality of resources available are the results of policy.

Homelessness may be a crucial problem for families in some areas, while in others, good relationships with the housing department may result in this area of work being appropriately dealt with by housing officers. Liaison with education may result in truancy being largely dealt with by the education welfare officers, liberal use of pastoral care, school refuges for truants both inside school and within the remedial education framework; close co-operation over multi-problem families may be the norm. Alternatively in your area you may find most truancy problems result in court action and considerable work in supplying social enquiry reports to the court.

Policy towards ethnic minorities may include well developed community relations and positive discrimination in selecting staff for residential establishments who will reflect the ethnic balance of the community, or of the residents to be cared for. Interpreters, language courses and schemes to help children from non-English-speaking homes can all facilitate harmonious community provision.

There are variations of policy reflected inside the department itself too. Neighbouring authorities frequently have very different proportions of children in care; for example, Bedfordshire has 7.0 per 1,000 and Hertford 4.9 per 1,000; Cornwall 5.4 per 1,000 and Devon 7.5 per 1,000 (DHSS 1982a). Some areas refuse more applications for children to be received into care than they accept; in others, the reverse is true (Packman 1975).

Under Section 1(1) of the Child Care Act 1980 financial help may be offered 'in exceptional circumstances' to diminish the need to receive children into care or bring them before the court. In one authority this may mean that a social worker may spend up to £5 on any one family, but any subsequent expenditure requires the consent of the social services committee, whereas in another authority, while the social worker has no authority over expenditure herself, authority for spending up to £300 lies within the powers of the area team.

In seeking to understand your authority's interpretation of policy, try not only to visit the various establishments and services, but to share your opinion of them with colleagues who have used them. Renewing your perspectives with incoming social workers can challenge the unquestioning assumptions into which we can all easily slide.

Questions about inter-agency policy

Housing: What help is offered by the housing department to enable children to be discharged from care? For children going out of care at 18? To enable families to foster a sibling group? How is the responsibility for homeless families handled?

Education: Is there liaison with magistrates and education departments about policy for truants? Is there a special provision for those aged over 15 who truant? What quality and kinds of special education are available? What 'out of school' education is there? Remedial? Attached to Intermediate Treatment projects? Home tutors?

Health: What liaison facilities are there between social, education and health services? Does the area team meet with health visitors to discuss community problems? Communication problems?

Leisure and recreation: What facilities are specifically geared to deprived families? Which ethnic and age groups are catered for?

What liaison is there with the Intermediate Treatment programme? *Community relations*: What ethnic groups are reflected? Does each of these have a specialist officer? What advice facilities are available to my department?

Intra-agency questions: What 'support' systems are available for families? Home helps? Family aides? Meals on wheels? Transport? Tenants' associations? Community groups? Drop-ins? Craft workshops? Is there a volunteer organiser linked to your area? Is decision-making delegated to a level that frees workers to have some autonomy and does that include the administration of finance? What are the policies regarding Intermediate Treatment and fostering? What kinds of day and residential care does the authority have? Are the establishments staffed to a level that enables positive work to take place? Are they supported in forming programmes of assessment and treatment for the children? What formal and informal channels of communication are there between the fieldworkers and the directorate?

Posterity

How much to record of your assessment is always an acute conflict between recognising that 'posterity' (your colleagues next week, next year, in five years, or the child in care in several years' time) may need the crucial clues you have unearthed, and the severe constraints of time and inclination.

The reason and source of referral, family components and addresses and telephone numbers are likely to form part of your basic recording for your agency. Beyond that you face the difficulties of judgement and personal prejudice in comments on what people look, dress and sound like, yet these can be important outward signs of internal changes. Risk committing your views to paper – you can revise the word pictures later and often pick up improvements in family conditions, attitudes and self-care that you might otherwise have missed.

In assessing small children knowledge of separations from their parents and their milestones of development will be essential for all decision-making. Note interactions between parents and children of all ages and observe their body language as well as what they say. Record anything unusual.

Try to sort out your recording under fact, opinion and assumptions. Make clear what is based on information and from whom, and what is based on observation – your own or someone else's.

Your level of recording will reflect the purpose of the assessment but there are some basic questions related to any written information kept about families and children.

Questions about posterity

1. Do the family understand that I will be keeping records? Do they, and I, know who will have access to these records?
2. Do the family understand why I need the information I request?
3. Have I found out and recorded a detailed description of the specific problem, the behaviour patterns associated with it, the way in which each member of the family is affected by it, the way in which each handles it?

Place

Choosing where to do interviews will depend a great deal on their purpose and on the overall policy of your area team. If your interviewing rooms are the size of broom cupboards, as mine were at one stage, you will not do many office interviews! Family interviews away from home will depend on sensitivity to how much financially and emotionally it costs the family to travel, and, for example, what care can be offered for the needs of the 18-month-old. A home visit may carry the message of inspection with it, or offend family mores, but it can also be a useful tool in revealing, in non-verbal ways, complexities of relationship that may take far longer to discover in office settings. Parents may present themselves one way to residential staff at the establishment and quite another at home; their relationship with their children in their own home will be different too.

In hospital, worried and possibly guilty about the injury their child has received, however it occurred, parents' defences and anger are often very different from their responses at home, or in an office setting. If you take a child out, or involve him in an activity, your assessment of his ability and responsiveness is likely to be different from one based solely on a formal interview.

Questions about place

1. What will the place I have chosen to see him in say to the child? His parents? Day or residential staff? The court? Is that the message I want to give? Does the choice of place need explanation?
2. Is the place in which I see the child upsetting relationships for

him? Would seeing the child or parents in another setting help my decision-making?

3. Is there a policy about where interviews are held? Do I need authority to alter this?

4. Are there available play materials? Toilet facilities? Space to separate family members if I need to?

5. Have I always seen this child, or these parents, in the same venue? Is it time I changed this?

People

Assessment is always a combination of viewpoints which have interacted with one another. Too often only one of these is presented in writing. In matrimonial welfare reports the reporter is required to present the views of all parties to the court. In assessment work all views should be recorded, even though you may have the decision to reach, and that decision reflects only one aspect of the case. Time is always an active constraint but the questions below are intended to help you focus on whether you know what you have left out, and whether you are sure of the reasons you have done so.

Questions about people.

1. Have I seen the child alone? With siblings? With parents? With peers? Involved in something he likes? In a formal setting? If not, do I know about the areas these would reveal from other sources? How can I discover them?

2. Have I seen the parents/child minder/foster parents/adopters together and separately? In their own home and in the office? If their verbal skills are limited have I offered them and myself the opportunity to communicate in other ways – drama, drawing, interpreters?

3. Have I consulted the following where appropriate? – our own clerical staff (including receptionist), family aides, home help, health visitor, GP, psychiatrist, educational psychologist, teacher, child minders, foster parents, residential staff, day care staff, other social workers who have had contact, e.g. hospital social workers, child guidance staff? Community relations officer, ethnic minority adviser, self-help groups?

4. Do the family know whom I want to contact and why?

5. Where the community situation plays a significant part, have the family consulted tenants' associations, community groups, housing, welfare rights? Have I told them how to?

Expectations

In each assessment that you undertake it is wise to clarify with your supervisor what expectations you each have of the task. At the end of this chapter there is an assessment check-list which it may help you to go through together. Where there are several children in the family, you may need to treat each one individually, but this would depend on the purpose of your assessment. As weaknesses are often recorded in detail and strengths not mentioned, try underlining strengths in one colour and causes for concern in another.

Talking of strengths and weaknesses, it is worth reminding you (and myself) that no one remembers everything during interviews, or knows all the answers to clients' questions. Clients return to important areas, provided we remain receptive. They prefer us to say honestly 'I don't know but I'll find out', or 'I'm sorry, I'd forgotten about that', than to invent the answer. The main thing is to be reliable in finding out and giving them the information you promised and in treating the knowledge you receive about the family as confidential and thus requiring your respect. Your clients need to be able to have confidence in you, so appearing rushed and over-burdened will simply waste your interview time, as they will find it difficult to share with you. The defences this evokes will alter how both you and the problem are perceived; either 'it is too small a difficulty for *you* to bother about', or 'it is far worse than whatever you've come from, so you will have to deal with my probem first, won't you?'

Remember, too, that your supervisor can only be as good as the degree of trust you show towards her. Prepare for supervision by keeping notes of the feelings you want to discuss, as well as the facts that you need to find out about.

All of this is part of your basic equipment, rather than specific to child care. My hope is that the six 'Ps' and the questions outlined in this chapter will help you to plan your interviews while the check-list can serve as a reminder for what may get left out in your early considerations.

Check-list 1 – *Assessment*

Family: Who constitutes the family unit? Who gets left out and why? Ages of all members, cultural background, employment, job satisfaction; marriage status of all members, date parents were married (if they were), marriage satisfaction for each partner. Description of each family member and their relationships with each other. Parents' capacity to parent the children? Siblings substituting for parents? Other role transfers?

History: Parents' own background, each child's history, including all separations, alternative carers, significant events; any history of frequent moves or job changes? Significance?

Accommodation: What kind? What facilities? How maintained? What impact on family life? Who likes it and who doesn't? How involved are the family with their neighbours, the local shops, the community?

Physical factors: Eating habits, type and sufficiency of food, clothing, bedding, level of cleanliness and its importance to the family, heating, fuel used and level of economy.

Finances: Income and debts, including payments under court orders. Any problems? How will your assessment and its outcome affect them? How comfortable are the family about discussing money?

Health: Any problems? Has child reached physical 'milestones' appropriately (Sheridan 1975)? Has there been a history for any family member of ill health, hospital or continued anxiety about health?

Leisure: Who enjoys doing what? Is this an area for development or advice?

Attitudes: Towards their own social/racial/community position; towards each other; to the reason for social work involvement; to sharing with a social worker; to involvement of other help; to day care or residential staff; to authority; to education; to religion, their own or others'?

Child: Are his needs being met within the family group? Can they be met while living with the family? If removed from the family? How does he see the family and his role in it? Does he want to remain part of it? Is he fulfilling his potential? What is his capacity for play, for learning, for self-preservation, for sharing? Does he panic, disrupt others' activities, mix well with a group, follow or lead? Who does he depend on? Does he communicate verbally or in other ways? Can he express his feelings? How? Is he aggressive physically or verbally? How does he deal with stress? How does he cope with frustration or control? With his feelings of love and hate? How does he see himself physically and emotionally? What are his goals for himself?

Other agencies: Health, education or housing involvement? Work opportunities? Any other agencies in contact? Their role? Family's view of them?

Conclusions: Reasons for them, on what they are based, and what constraints have influenced them. Do they conflict with the family, child's or other agency's wishes? How will any conflicts be resolved?

2 Prevention or Enabling?

There were no powers for the local authorities to undertake preventive work with families and children through the children's departments until the passing of the Children and Young Persons Act 1963. They simply had a duty to investigate and discover whether children needed to come into care. The Act was regarded as revolutionary, giving the statutory right to work with families before the crisis of reception into care, and it was expected to result in a considerable diminution of the numbers of children coming into care. In fact, in the first three years after its inception those numbers *increased*. It is speculated that this was brought about by the rise in numbers of families in need that came to the notice of the children's departments.

The Child Care Act 1980 brought together much of the previous legislation. Section 1 of that Act makes it 'the duty of every local authority to make available such advice, guidance and assistance as may promote the welfare of children, by diminishing the need to receive children into, or keep them in care . . . or bring them before the juvenile court'. The local authority can do this by providing 'assistance in kind, or in exceptional circumstances, in cash'.

There has been some concern expressed about the wording of the Section (Hudson 1980) as it is suggested that this encourages the presumption that a child's welfare is diminished in residential care. Delays in the decision for a child to come into care may result in him becoming more disturbed. Social service departments need to be encouraged to focus on promotion of welfare, on what Parker (1980) calls 'enablement', rather than prevention. This includes enabling a child to come into care at the optimum moment, that he may remain in care for the shortest possible time. If he needs more help than his family can give, it is a positive decision to receive a child into care, provided that a clear treatment plan, which the whole family understands, is formulated at the point of transfer of care.

It is in the field of preventive work that the skills of assessment are most critical. The outline in Chapter 1 may be undertaken by field, day or residential social workers, and ideally should include the skills and knowledge of all three, within a multi-disciplinary team. There is an increasing use of day facilities in which teams of social workers, teachers, doctors, educational and clinical psychologists, and psychiatrists assess the needs of whole family groups or of individual children, and form treatment plans. In some instances it has been a change of management policy that has brought about the move from residential assessment of children, separated from their families, to day assessment in which their families are involved. In other areas, residential workers in assessment centres have initiated the use of their facilities on a day basis, involving families more directly in their work. In a few enterprising area teams, individuals have pursued the realisation that children can, in many instances, be better assessed without removing them from home, and have co-ordinated the various skills from health, education and residential social work to compile a full assessment, and called a case conference to discuss the implications of the findings.

Let's look in more detail at one of the areas that determine your goals for work with families in the community or a child's need to be received into care.

Kellmer Pringle (1974) defines the four basic needs of children as:

1. Love and security – a relationship with an adult whom they can trust, who gives them a feeling of being loved and worthy of love, and who is himself enjoying a rewarding relationship with another. Love includes care for the physical development of the child and the ability to offer an environment in which a child can grow physically and emotionally. Love is given without expecting return. Security includes the need for familiar places and objects, a known routine, consistent attitudes and behaviour towards and around a child. It acknowledges the child's right to idiosyncratic rituals, and encourages knowledge of a past and a future as confirming individual identity.

2. New experiences – the opportunity to explore the world in which he lives and to discover its range. For the baby this may be varying textures and toys and the opportunity for rolling on the floor, for the teenager it may be use of youth facilities to test himself out in strenuous outdoor actitivies, but for both the vital ingredients are play and language. A lack of these is likely to lead to 'passivity, fearfulness, frustration or irritability'.

3. Praise and recognition – this is the medium by which a child is enabled to develop a capacity for learning. In being recognised as doing something well, in being encouraged in some simple skill, the child is also learning who he is and where he can contribute to the world around him. The appropriate handling of mistakes, mishaps,

mischief and misdemeanours are the areas to assess.

4. Responsibilty – the need for even the youngest child to understand the responsibility he has for his own actions is an important facet of maturation starting with self-care, doing it himself, choice of friends, etc. Sadly it is often the missing factor for children in care, as responsibility is not given to them for decisions about their own lives, and they then leave care unable to exercise adult responsibility in decision-making. Giving independence does not mean failing to offer guidance or limits. It requires differentiation between disapproval of the child's action and rejection of the child himself, reflecting the Christian concept of loving the sinner while hating the sin. The adult's role is to give the advice the child needs in order to make an informed decision.

Following your assessment, your first question should be 'For *this* child, are there enough new experiences, love and security, praise and recognition and responsibility?' 'Enough' will reflect policy, in that your agency may tolerate a less satisfactory parenting situation at home, either where it has particularly good resources for working on a preventive basis, or where its own provision is also unsatisfactory. 'Enough' is also a subjective qualitative factor that needs to be carefully tested with your supervisor, in order that it does not merely mirror your own experiences. 'Is there enough for this particular child' is the emphasis of your question, for the child is your client. The parents may need help under various other forms of legislation, for example they may be mentally or physically ill or handicapped, but in your responsibilities under the child care legislation you are required to consider the child's welfare. The most common mistake in child care work occurs when this is lost sight of in the interests of keeping families together, or not hurting or upsetting the adult concerned.

The second question to ask is 'Is there a capacity or willingness to change?' Without this, years of work may be wasted and children left in situations that become increasingly inappropriate and intolerable, particularly when they reach adolescence.

If your conclusion is that there is 'enough', then the third question, in today's climate of economic pressures, should be 'Do I need to be involved?' Where you identify a family in need, in the widest sense, then preventive, or rather enabling, work should be based on clearly defined goals. The work may draw upon the skills of family therapy, self-help groups, or day care. Casework community work and groupwork all offer models for this kind of enabling; much will depend on your local resources and personal skills.

Uses of Section 1

The following brief outline of some of the uses that have been made of Section 1 of the Child Care Act 1980 is intended to stimulate your imagination about preventive measures, and not to set the pattern of what should be done. Negotiations with outside agencies and policy within will have a direct bearing on how you may use the powers within the legislation. It is now taken for granted that social workers will negotiate on behalf of their less able clients with such agencies as the DHSS and fuel boards and other council departments. The power to do this in respect of families is derived from Section 1 and can be delegated to a grant-aided voluntary organisation, for example a welfare rights advice office. In assessment work consider the family's capacity to negotiate for themselves. One of your goals might be to increase this ability in the family.

Prevention of reception into care through homelessness

Work in this area has included the notorious provision of bed and breakfast accommodation for families in hotels, which is less costly financially and emotionally than receiving children into care but places the family under a lot of pressure. Usually there are no cooking facilities and many of the hotels require guests to be out during the day. Use of day-care facilities in a flexible and imaginative way can considerably reduce pressure for these families.

Rents can be guaranteed by social services, and this may include an arrangement with the family that social services will pay £1 for every £1 that the family pay off their rent arrears. This encourages the family to continue to accept responsibility for their own defaulting on payment. Use has been made, in some areas, of short-life property that is to be demolished as part of the housing departments' development plans. These properties are likely to be in poor condition and include many stressful factors, but they do leave the family with greater autonomy than they have in a continuing hotel placement. Since the 1977 Housing Act the majority of the work with homeless families is undertaken by the housing department. However, there is still a preventive role for social services to play as the figures for reception in care in 1979 demonstrate. In England and Wales 500 children were received into care that year because they were homeless or evicted (Department of Health and Social Security 1982a).

Fuel cut-offs

In addition to the negotiations undertaken with gas and electricity boards, there are still some situations in which local authorities have paid fuel bills or, alternatively, have lent bottled gas equipment for lighting, cooking or heating.

Equipment provision

Bedding, cookers, fires and furniture are often provided for low-income families, but obviously negotiation with the local DHSS is crucial. In some areas preventive work may include the provision of cots, play-pens, stair gates, double 'buggies' or prams, if these cannot be obtained from other sources. Often application to local charities can be successful in meeting these types of need.

Welfare promotion

Day care for school children during the holidays and after school is a growing need. A few authorities run play centres but too little is being attempted in this field. Holiday schemes for children are still under-funded and under-valued when one compares the provision made by the French Colony holiday movement. Nearly every child in France goes on a colony holiday at some time during its childhood. Colonies aim to mix children from different backgrounds and give every child the experience of structured, imaginative play, adults as friends, and the opportunity of finding that every child is good at something and capable of giving to another. The adults running colonies receive a brief residential training (which, incidentally, has much to offer a beginning residential social worker). This incorporates learning by doing in a range of skills, including drama, crafts, games, singing, exploring the environment, safely balancing a daily programme and responsibility for a group of children together.

In France much of the finance for Colonies is derived from industry. In England the Council for Colony Holidays for School-children (CCHS)* runs holidays for about 3,000 children a year, but the financing of these is still largely a matter to negotiate for each individual family. About 15 per cent of the children sent are sponsored by local authority education or social service departments. Funds can also be raised from charities.

* CCHS, Linden Manor, Upper Colwall, Malvern, Worcs.

Other schemes that have been promoted by Section 1 funds in urban areas, to reduce isolation, are the growing number of family groups, where the elderly, whose families have moved away, are linked with young families who have no grandparents nearby. There is a need, too, for increase in the number of 'drop-ins' for adolescents and single parents, places for informal counselling and peer group sharing. Promotion of baby-sitting circles and bulk buying schemes, a part of the earliest form of community work, still contribute to increased community links for families where parents or children are isolated.

Preventing children coming into care because their parents are ill
In addition to the provision of home helps and family aides through council schemes, it is possible under Section 1 to offer the family the means to pay for private help in the home. This can be either on a home-help or a living-in nanny basis. (See check-list 2 for areas that need resolving in using this form of assistance for families.)

Cash grants
The most frequent use of Section 1 is the small cash grant made to tide a family over. The study undertaken by Michael Hill and Peter Laing in 1977 (Hill and Laing 1979) showed that by far the most common use of Section 1 payments was for food, closely followed by grants for fuel costs.

Decision-making
Usually the power to agree to a Section 1 payment will lie with your supervisor, the senior, or team leader, but in some authorities this will be at a very limited level, e.g. £10. In a few instances decisions about payments still lie with the social services committttees. You will need to establish your own authority's policy and delegation in this matter.

How you give cash, or food, or make payments on behalf of clients needs to be carefully thought out in relation to that family's pattern of behaviour and to form part of an overall treatment policy. The dilemma for many social workers is that the families are trying to subsist on incomes that the social workers could not themselves manage to budget on. Increasingly there is a temptation to give cash grants to 'top-up' a family income.

A family that comes with some regularity on Fridays for cash grants needs to be confronted with the pattern and the causation fully explored. Continuing the pattern of dependency that this forms does not actually help them. It may be possible to identify with the family at what point in the week they were first aware of the need, as a step towards learning to re-budget. Sometimes it is better to invest a larger sum in getting the budgeting properly sorted out than to keep making small emergency payments, but this may require a series of interviews and assessment, rather than a simple payment.

Handing over money is often an uncomfortable role for a social worker. The discomfort may reflect guilt at your own relative wealth, but often it also reflects a change in role from the usual acceptance of the client, as he is, to a visible underlining of the client's inadequacy. Try not to delegate the actual handing over of the money to your administrative staff. Remember the client needs you to acknowledge his feelings at the moment of receiving the money, and to know that he still has dignity and the right to choose how to spend that grant.

Intermediate Treatment and the 'continuum of care'

Preventing children coming before the juvenile court and, when the child appears, recommending alternatives to residential care, are both part of the preventive task. The variety of reasons for which a child may be brought before the juvenile court need not be detailed here (see Leeding 1980, Chapter 8, or Hoggett 1977, Chapter 4). In care proceedings neither a supervision order nor a care order can be made unless the court is satisfied that the child will not receive care and control without being the subject of an order. The exception to this is in the case of an offence having been committed, which in an adult court would be punishable by imprisonment.

Social workers are often accused by police and magistrates of being too lenient about delinquency, wanting the youngsters who have committed offences to 'get off' with inappropriate sentences. Against this should be weighed the evidence of David Thorpe's study of 132 children who were the subject of care orders to one local authority following criminal proceedings. Some 83.2 per cent of the care orders had been recommended by social workers, although one-third of the children had no previous court appearance.

Children committed to care, following a court appearance for delinquency, see care as punishment and their 'sentence', often intended as an enabling experience, as unjust because of its length. A care order for a 14-year-old is likely to result in two years in residential care, followed by two years' supervision while 'home on trial' – a four-year 'sentence' for what may be a minor offence.

The Children and Young Persons Act 1969 includes provision for a supervision order (Section 12 (2)) with the possibility of requiring a youngster to attend an Intermediate Treatment facility. Intermediate Treatment is conceived as that which comes between preventive work and residential care. It can include, under the Criminal Law Act 1977, a residential requirement or attendance of ninety days or less. The original objective (see *Children in trouble* (Home Office 1968)) was the decriminalisation of young offenders, with considerable emphasis on their deprivation, which was seen as the underlying cause of much juvenile delinquency.

Paley and Thorpe (1974) suggest a 'continuum of care' as an approach to recognising a delinquent youngster's needs (see Table 2.1). They propose a table of all the resources a local authority provides, from those generally available to full-time care. If you chart your own local authority's resources in this way and consider a child's needs against the table, you can see what provision you should be recommending to the court. This should help to avoid some of the 'tariff' system of each offence requiring a greater punishment than the one before, with a swift movement from failure in attendance at one kind or preventive provision, into residential care, detention centres and Borstals.

There has been a strong bid made for the separation of the delinquent and non-delinquent in Intermediate Treatment schemes, and for the focus of resources to be on preventing delinquents entering institutional care (Thorpe *et al.* 1980b). Despite this, many authorities open their Intermediate Treatment schemes to youngsters with whom the social workers are involved on a preventive basis, following the rationale of the original White Paper and as presented by Kerslake and Jones (1979).

'Latchkey' provision, for children before and after school and during school holidays, for those whose parents work, can be seen as typical of schemes that are preventive of both the need for children to be in residential care and of the likelihood of delinquency. There have been some imaginative self-help projects in this field, like Gingerbread Corner (Willmott and Mayne 1980).

A 'treatment' group may involve a wide range of activities or be for discussion and problem-sharing only. Groups are run by various combinations of local authority social workers, probation officers, education welfare officers, housing officers, youth officers and police. The 'therapeutic community' would aim to

Table 2.1 A 'continuum of care'*

Provision type	Type of child/problem for whom it may be appropriate (add your own variations)
1. Youth clubs, uniformed groups, evening classes, adult education, sports clubs, crafts, music.	Child who lacks concept of self-worth, adults to stimulate interests, sense of community, is bored.
2. 'Latchkey' provision, drop-in centres, work experience schemes.	Child/family's problem is related to use of time and place, being alone, having no goal for the future.
3. Remedial education on or off school site. Specialist youth clubs, child guidance groups.	Specific problems where the family sees the solution as within reach if only . . .
4. Local 'treatment' groups, with a higher adult/youngster ratio than three.	Combined peer group and parental problems where 'sharing' is the next stage in development.
5. Treatment groups that include residential week-ends.	Peer group or parental problems where the child needs reinforcement of skills or confrontation at a more intensive level.
6. Treatment group that incorporates forty-five days' residential provision, beginning with at least one week in residence, followed by week-ends and further residential weeks.	Separation from previous patterns of behaviour is seen as crucial for a new beginning, followed by reinforcement through pleasurable participation.
7. Local intensive treatment group with specialist social workers. Youngster attends three nights a week and three week-ends out of four. May include work with a parallel parent group.	Education/work are being maintained but leisure use reflects acute problems for parents and child.
8. Ninety days in a 'therapeutic community' with intensive supervision.	New learning and skills need to be established and new concepts of self reinforced for previous behaviour to cease. There is likely to be family reinforcement of previous behaviour patterns which will need to be resisted.
9. Full-time day care, with parallel parent groups.	Problem of long standing. Child's removal may reinforce the pattern of the way that the family copes with problems, or result in a loss of the family for the child.
10. Full residential care.	Child is a danger to self or to the community. He has educational or medical needs that cannot be met in the community. A continuing place in his family is not available or suitable; he needs to be out of the home.

* Based on table in Paley and Thorpe (1974).

show the young person the way his behaviour affects others. A good example of this can be seen in the Northampton Weldon Centre featured in the DHSS film *Intermediate Treatment in action*. The workers seek to increase the child's range of skills and understanding about himself, while fostering his self-esteem. In particular, the child's responsibility for his own action and choices would be demonstrated. Consistency in handling by the staff group is an essential tool in the treatment. Indeed, as Adams *et al*. (1981) point out, 'Intermediate Treatment represents not so much a method of working with the young as an attitude towards them'.

Where delinquency has been a motivating factor in the request for you to undertake an assessment with a family, it is obviously important to consider the role of the Intermediate Treatment officers of your authority. If your Intermediate Treatment facilities are limited (they are actually still non-existent in some authorities twelve years after the Children and Young Persons Act 1969), it may be helpful to involve your youth service or careers advisers in any plans you may wish to formulate.

The biggest problem in all this work is time. Courts are likely to give you three weeks in which to decide a child and family's future life structure. Co-ordinating the various crucial people in the scenario can be frustrating or impossible. You may have to draw conclusions from scanty evidence. If you do, then say so. If you are then given a further role with the family use the first few weeks to clarify your assessment and formulate goals.

Conclusion

Your task with a family is to draw together all the factors of your assessment (see check-list 1) and to consider the way in which the child's needs are, or are not, being met in the home situation. Look for and list the causes for concern and the sources of strength that you perceive. Consider sharing that list with the family. It will include the family's own potential and the resources within the community appropriate to the needs discerned. Which of those resources can your authority offer and what degree of priority do the causes of concern warrant? The answer to this lies in the spectrum of cases for which your area team is responsible.

I would suggest that ideally you should aim at listing what you consider the child and family needs and then give the conflicts of priorities and policies. For example, full day care may be appropriate for a particular 4-year-old and his family's needs, but not be available owing to a policy of limiting this provision. The priority for you to remain involved in preventive casework may be increased because of the lack of appropriate resources, or you may identify the need for a self-help group and be able to stimulate its growth. However, unless the conflicts of policy and need are identified in this way it is difficult to gather the necessary evidence to effect change in policy. Prevention and enabling, at its best, includes effecting changes in policy and priorities to reflect the needs of the community you serve.

Check-list 2 – *Prevention*

Before planning for a child to be received or committed to care, have I:
1. Evaluated the child's needs? Is there a way for him to receive 'enough': (a) love and security; (b) new experiences; (c) praise and recognition; (d) responsibility, without coming into residential care? If so, for how long?
2. Discovered the child's wishes? Are they based on fact or fantasy?
3. Considered the benefits/risks of: (a) staying at home – physical, emotional, educational; (b) alternative provision – 'continuum' day care; (c) reception into care – conflicts, family identity and position, types of provision?

Alternatives to short-term care: If planning short-term care (e.g. while mother is confined or in hospital) there are certain specific factors to consider. Have I checked that the following alternatives would not meet the need more appropriately?
1. Relatives'/friends' care instead. If no, is the reason money? (See 6).
2. Day care + home help + voluntary help + parent change hours worked.
3. Letter to parent's employer re: (a) extra holiday; (b) time off without pay.
4. Application made to DHSS for parent's loss of earnings to be met at supplementary benefit level.
5. Child be admitted to hospital with parent.
6. Section 1 payment under Child Care Act 1980 for: (a) parent's loss of earnings; (b) relative to care for child; (c) daily minder to care for child; (d) paid help to move into the household.

If arranging alternative care, have I checked the following:
1. That parents' whereabouts during the day are known to the caring adult and to the social worker? How can the parents be contacted?
2. Times of collection and delivery of children to day nursery, school or daily minder. Are these known to both the parents and to the person who will be doing them? Who will contact whom if the child does not come as expected?
3. If the helper is to sleep in, what are the bedroom arrangements? Is there enough bedding?
4. If there is to be payment to a 'nanny' or similar, does the arrangement include her food? Clarify what is included and what is not.

5. Household management – who will do the: (a) washing; (b) shopping; (c) cleaning, with the money from whom?

6. Is the gas or electricity cut off? What alternatives need arranging?

7. Would the home help, family aide, volunteer or nanny need any special equipment?

8. How long can the alternative care cope for? Have I set a date to review the arrangements?

3 Day Care and the Under 5s

This is the 'Cinderella' of many mixed case-loads. As parents seek to improve, or maintain, their standards of living the need for both parents to work has increased, resulting in a higher proportion of children being cared for during the day by people other than their own parents. Maternity leave is now a statutory option for mothers. This makes it harder for them to recognise the real choice involved in leaving their children with others. The social work task may be to help them to make a choice, rather than automatically returning to work because their job has been kept open for them. Despite the recognition given to theories of loss and separation on social work training courses (see Bowlby 1973, and Rutter 1972 and 1975), it is still remarkably easy for these to be forgotten when faced with the day-to-day pressures of a busy local authority social services department – and this is particularly likely to occur in the field of day care for the under 5s.

The responsibility for nursery provision and supervision of the day care of the under 5s was transferred from the health services to the social services in April 1971. The re-drawing of many of the local authority boundaries and the Local Authorities Social Services Act implementing the Seebohm Report had brought reorganization and confusion. Recommendations for an increase in nursery and education provision for under 5s had been made, but these were delayed while the new authorities became accustomed to their wider range of responsibilities. The need for close co-ordination between the three main strands of provision – health, education and social services – has been slowly recognised, and many local authorities have a committee that ensures that planning and development is shared. None the less, it is important to recognise the continuing and separate roles of each.

Education

Since the 1944 Education Act the local authority education department has had a 'duty to regard the need for provision for Under Fives'. Plowden recommended in 1967 that nursery education on a part-time basis should be available for 50 per cent of 3-year-olds and 90 per cent of those over 4. Implementation of this began in 1973, but the recent cuts in government expenditure have resulted in many of the planned expansion programmes being dropped.

While nursery schools appear to make little difference to a child's subsequent IQ or educational progress after primary school, they do enable children from non-English-speaking homes to make full use of education earlier in their formal school careers. They are also seen by many parents as offering a helpful beginning to school. In their present format they do not solve the problem of children who need day care in order that their parents may both be in full-time employment, as the majority are part-time places. Many schools feel that two and a half hours is a long enough separation from the parent and that by having two sessions daily they are able to offer the provision to a wider range of parents. Some nursery schools accept children from day nurseries, or minders; however, as both Tizared *et al.* (1976) and Ferri (1977) point out, children are best able to benefit from educational opportunites if these are integrated in nursery centres where day care and pre-school education are combined.

Health

The health authorities' responsibility for the pre-school child remains that of advice and monitoring progress. The health visitor is often the key professional in the care of the under-5-year-old, but she no longer has the statutory responsibility for placement in day care. In many authorities the right of the health visitor to place children has been retained, but this can lead to a lack of information for the day nursery or family centre staff, or to confusion for the social workers who supervise the child minders. Equally, failure to inform the health visitor of a child's placement in day care can make it very difficult for her to follow up the child's health.

Some health clinics have opened part-time crèches as a way of encouraging mothers to bring their children to clinics, providing a community resource for them while they do their shopping. Such crèches have the additional advantage of helping young mothers to share anxieties and problems. Links between clinics and daily minders have also been established and some authorities running courses for minders have found it helpful, where there is provision for the children to play, to base these in clinic premises.

Social services

The wide range of social services' responsibilities in the field of the under 5s is often shared between different administrative divisions of the department, and so some authorities have appointed a co-ordinator for all services for the under 5s. The common division of service lies between the provision of public services, on premises other than in a private home, and those provided in someone's own home. Nurseries, play-groups, 1 o'clock clubs, mother and toddler groups and crèches may all be supervised or co-ordinated by one division while the child minders may be the responsibility of another. This can be a strength, drawing on skills in resource management, staff selection, training and support on the one hand and the skills of assessment of family dynamics and needs on the other. Sadly the result is often that the fieldworker remains lacking in knowledge and understanding of the strengths and problems of the nursery and other day care provision. I would postulate that it is not possible to do an acceptable level of assessment of a family's need for day care provision without detailed knowledge of your own authorities' resources. To help you find out what the parents should expect you to know, I have listed for each type of provision the sort of questions you should be able to answer about it.

Day nurseries

These may be provided by the local authority, run for the profit of the owners, or set up by charitable trusts such as the NSPCC or the Save the Children Fund. There are also some community-owned nurseries. Parents arrange for children to go to the privately run ones themselves, although in exceptional circumstances it is possible for the local authority to pay the fees for a child to attend (under the Child Care Act 1980, Section 1). Private nurseries have to register with the local authority and their standards of safety, space, health, hygiene, diet, play stimulus and staffing ratio are all monitored by the authority. Responsibility for this may lie in either day care or fieldwork divisions. Access to places in the voluntary or community-based nurseries will vary. Some are based on local authority assessment of need, some on the nursery's own assessment, and some will accept applications from social workers, GPs, health visitors or parents.

Most nurseries are open fifty-one weeks of the year, from early morning (some open at 7 a.m.) to early evening (usually about 6 p.m.). A proportion of the staff will be trained in the care of under 5s and the premises, because they are for a group of children, are unlikely to make parents feel anxious about the standard of their own homes. Many nurseries still expect little of the parent except regular delivery of their child (in a clean condition), to be told of any major incident that affects the child's life, and to have the child collected on time. Gradually the nursery involvement with parents is increasing. Some now have mothers' groups, either in the evenings or during the day, to help mothers learn social skills like cooking, sewing or budgeting, or child-care skills such as feeding or appropriate play.

Even the best-run nurseries have staff changes, illness and annual leave which mean that each child is likely to experience care from several of the nursery nurses. Some establishments offer student nursery nurse training, and move the students around from group to group of children without recognising the impact on the children concerned: the loss of the mother substitute the student may represent.

The advantages of the nursery to the child can be in either compensatory or supplementary care. Children from poor housing, inadequate parenting, or who have developmental handicaps will benefit from the compensatory skilled care, regular food, and a warm, clean, light, stimulating environment. The beginnings of educational and socialisation opportunities of the nursery, including sand, water and the larger toys, offer supplementary care to the child of parents who wish to return to work. Despite all this, social workers need to remember what they know about loss and separation anxiety (Bowlby 1973) when they are assessing children's needs and their parents' wants.

At this point money rears its head. For many parents, in many local authorities, the cost for their child at a day nursery will be far less than any other form of full-time day care. Some wiser authorities assess parental means and arrange that they pay the same rate for day care in whatever form this is provided. The authority then pays the fees to the minder, play-group, private nursery, etc. and collects the parents' contributions in the same way as it does for nursery care.

Sometimes officers in charge of nurseries find themselves acting as 'debt collectors' with parents. This frustrates their attempts to involve the parents more widely in the management and use of the nursery.

Finally, I would endorse Tizard's (1978) recommendation for nursery services:

1. They should meet the needs of children emotionally and socially. Continuity of staff involved with any one child, and a warm and safe physical environment that is attractive to both children and

staff, are essential elements. Young children need to be in small groups.

2. They should be locally based, preferably near the parental home, or at least near their place of employment. It should not involve crossing a busy road, and should be within pram-pushing distance, with a toddler in tow.

3. They should include an educational provision, so that it is not necessary for the children to go out to nursery school.

4. The children's health should be cared for as part of the service, and a health visitor and doctor specialising in child health should call regularly. Ideally the nursery should be an infant welfare centre including a surgery for primary medical care.

5. They should be free, or at least the educational part of the day should be provided free, even if the extra time before and after school day is costed.

6. They should involve the parents in participation in the management as part of the agreement to their use of a place for their child.

What you need to know about your authority's nurseries
The nursery itself

Where each one is, and how it is reached by public transport. When it is open. How long its holidays are. What the cost is, and how it is worked out; does the parent pay the nursery staff or the town hall? How long the waiting list is for each nursery (they may differ, due to demographic patterns). Whether there is education provided at the nursery, or whether the children can/do go out to nursery school from the nursery. Whether the nursery includes outdoor play facilities; do the children go out to the park or shops?

Staff

How many are there? How many qualified and how many students? Are all the staff on the same pay scale, or are there discrepancies/difficulties? How do staff view (a) late arrivals and late collections; (b) infectious diseases; (c) feeding problems; (d) soiling problems? How do staff think these difficulties would affect the group of children?

Parents

Are parents (a) invited into the group rooms freely; (b) involved in the management of the nursery; (c) involved in fund raising for the nursery? Are there any groups for parents? How many attend? What are they for? When are they held?

Children
How many children are there? Is there a specific ratio of babies to toddlers? What is the youngest they will accept? Do they operate a baby room and groups-by-ages policy, a mixed age range on a family basis, or a combination of these systems? Can school age siblings come to the nursery in the holidays? On what grounds? What is the mixture of ethnic/cultural/social groups? What reasons govern allocation of places – are a particular number of children there because of suspected abuse, problem families, single parents. etc.? How many children are from 'normal' homes?

Private and voluntary nurseries – what you need to know in addition to above
Who in your authority supervises the nursery? Who knows it well? How are places gained or allocated?

Family centres
A more recent development in the field of day care is family centres. The usual aim of these is to mix full-time care of the child with some care for the parents. Some of the staff may be qualified social workers, psychologists, teachers, or psychotherapists in training, any of whom may undertake a programme of work with the parents and children together. Many of those referred to family centres have long-standing problems in forming relationships. There are several family centres specialising in helping children 'at risk' or who have been abused. In some cases the parents may stay all day; in others, parents may still deliver and collect their children, as in a day nursery, and many range between the two, so that parents attend for two or three days a week while the child is at the centre full time.

The major advantage of the family centre is that it enables the relationship between parent and child to continue. For many parents it offers an opportunity to regress and play with the childhood toys they did not have. For others it is their first experience of consistent daily caring, furnishing the possibility of personal growth. For the child the advantage comes in being able to explore new relationships while the familiar remains available. Many of the children also experience a new and more relaxed interaction with their parents while at the centre because the accountability for all that the child does is removed, and the parents are able to enjoy their children. Some family centres have extended their age groups and are working on a day-care basis with older children, for many of the family centre principles apply equally to long term preventive work with families. Family centres could be a valuable resource on your 'Continuum of Care' (see Table 2.1 p. 18).

What you need to know about family centres (in addition to nursery information)
What the staff aim to provide for the parents. The ethos for work with the parents, e.g. psycho-analytic? behavioural? task centred? The content of work with parents, e.g. one-to-one interviews? Groups? Shared skill learning? Reward systems? How many parents the staff are able to work with at one time. What the centre would want of a social worker already involved with a family.

Crèches

Crèches are available at some factories, hospitals and colleges of further education. They do not usually take children under 2. The child's place at the crèche is dependent on the parents' involvement with work, learning or a service and the place is conditional on the parent being available on the premises. The exception to this is the kind of crèche offered by the health clinic, and referred to previously.

Staffing ratios at crèches tend to be low, and play facilities do not always include outdoor opportunities. There are a number of trade union pressure groups at present urging that more crèches should be provided by employers. The Equal Opportunities Commission (1978) report stresses the need for provision for young children, in order that work may be a real choice for mothers.

What you need to know about crèches (in addition to the nursery questions)
Which employers offer them? What conditions attach to the place – e.g. can a parent have a day off work but the child still attend?

Mother and toddler groups and 1 o'clock clubs

For the under-2-year-old, where the relationship between parent and child is so crucial to subsequent development (Leach 1979), it is desirable that day care is a shared activity. This can still offer the parents some measure of relief from the pressure and demands of screaming children, while giving the child the opportunity to explore, with confidence engendered by the parents' presence.

Play-groups

The play-group movement has been the fastest growing development in day care for the under 5s. It offers part-time care of a child over 2 or $2\frac{1}{2}$ and gives the child a range of play opportunites that parents cannot afford in their own homes. Play-groups are often set up by mothers of children wanting a play-group for their own children. The Pre-school Playgroup Association offers training and advice to members. Sometimes parents are expected to be involved in some measure with the running of the group, whether in fund raising for equipment or in helping with the children on a rota basis. Many play-groups are grant-aided by local authorities and charge low fees for participation.

What you need to know about mother and toddler groups and play-groups (in addition to the nursery questions)
Who in your authority registers and supervises them? Who provides them, e.g. church, local authority, leisure and recreation department? What facilities do they provide? How much do parents have to be involved (a) while the children are there; (b) in the evenings; (c) in the running of it? How does a child get a place? Is there a waiting list? If it is out of doors, what happens when it rains?

Child minders

Opinions about child minders vary. There are the horror stories of children locked in cupboards or stood in line all day, but also tales of excellent care, where the minded child receives real substitute mothering. Research has confirmed that the most urgent need is for minders to receive support, stimulation, advice and additional facilities (Jackson, B. and S. 1979). It has also shown that the care minded children enjoy may be adequate physically, while leaving emotional needs unsatisfied (Mayall and Petrie 1977).

Many parents are prejudiced by press stories against the use of minders. Often the advantages of a minder have not been discussed with them and they feel threatened by the rivalry of relationship they anticipate. The minder–parent relationship needs a lot of care and thought from both parties, but when both are determined that the child's interests will be paramount, minding can provide the best and most natural care for a child whose parents have to go out to work.

Minders are often initially attracted to their job by their desire to earn a bit of money while staying at home with their own child. Few of them cost the exercise sensibly, forgetting the increase in wear and tear on their homes that two more under 5s will cause. The National Childminders Association is helping minders to get a more realistic payment scheme, and offers support groups and advice to those who want to start minding. It has negotiated a system of deduction and allowance for those minders who are on supplementary benefit.

Those who take other people's children into their homes, to care for them for more than two hours a day, for reward, are required to register as a child minder under the Nursery and Child Minders Act 1958. While most minders are women, the increase in one-parent families and of women working while their husbands stay at home has resulted in a few men being registered as child minders. For children who have no male figure in their lives this move can offer a great deal of help.

The Act gives little guidance on the standards for registration, although the DHSS has issued guidelines laying down minimum standards. As a field social worker with a mixed, demanding caseload it is easy to forget that it is the care of possibly fifty children or more for which you have undertaken responsibility when you vet a prospective minder. For this reason I commend the authorities that have separated out this task and developed a specialism of the registration and co-ordination of minders.

This field of work offers exciting opportunities for advising and supporting minders, and helping them to grow in their understanding of child development and stimulation. The mature and experienced minder becomes a much valued resource both for the community and the department.

What you should know about your own authority in relation to child minders
The criteria for registration
Do the health or housing departments have the right to veto? On what grounds? Does the fire officer have to visit – how much weight is given to his opinion? How is the decision not to register reached? Do we tell the reason? Write it? Give no reason? (All these occur in different authorities.) How long does registration take? Can a prospective minder start before registration is completed? On whose agreement? What is the local rate (average) for minders to charge?
Do we offer
A grant to minders when they register (to encourage registration and the purchase of equipment)? A playkit to minders on

registration? A training course – voluntary or compulsory? Details of when and where. Equipment on loan – lobster pot playpens, fireguards, stoveguards, double buggies, cots, stair gates etc.? A first-aid kit either issued or available cheaply to minders? A handbook for minders on first aid for children? A toy library? A mobile library that calls in the minder's area? A playbus that calls in their area? Any weekly groups for minders for support and sharing? A local group of the National Childminding Association 13 London Road, Bromley, Kent (tel. 01-464-6164)? An insurance policy for minders to take out for protection of themselves against claims on public liability or injury to the child in their care? A policy about holiday payments? A policy about numbers – is it different during the holidays? A registration kit containing leaflets on safety, diet, play and hygiene, care of Afro hair and skin, Asian diet, religious food differences, stationery for the minder to let you know when a child arrives or leaves a minder's care, record book for details of which children are being minded?

Are any of our minders
Salaried? If so, to which centre do they link? Paid a retainer, and paid extra for taking special children? Known as day foster parents or crisis carers? If so, what are the criteria for these?

Working with a prospective minder
Although a minder, like a foster parent, is offering a service, the field social worker's task remains one of assessment, at least until registration is completed, and even then the transition to colleague will be gradual as the minder's confidence and skill increases.

In assessing the suitability of the home, bear in mind the responsibility for other people's children when looking at the following: space, light, warmth and hygiene (including the care of their pets); safety, including stair gates, stoves, fires and windows; escape in the event of fire; fire extinguishers, fire blankets; play areas, including gardens and park; rest areas – beds, cots, playpens; toys and other play materials and the minder's understanding of them.

What style of parenting does the minder have with her own children? Permissive? Authoritarian? Controlling?

Does the minder understand the problems of: (a) rivalry between own and minded children; (b) rivalry between parent and minder; (c) children's development; (d) separation anxiety in children and the behaviour this causes?

What are the minder's views on: (a) ethnic/cultural/social

differences; (b) illness – physical, mental or in children; (c) strengths and weaknesses?

What kind of parenting did the minder herself receive? Has she 'come to terms' with it?

The minder should be encouraged, right from the start, to keep records – they hate having to do it as much as we do! – that give details of each child's name, age, home address, parents' name, address, place of employment, how to contact them during the day, someone with whom the minder can leave the child if the parent fails to collect him, the time of care offered (e.g. 8 a.m.–3.45 p.m.), what the care includes (e.g. all food, no washing, parent to supply disposable nappies), agreement about holidays for parents and minders, payment and alternative care where their holidays do not coincide, and what is to happen when the parent or minder is ill. Some departments now issue sample contracts and record books to their registered minders.

Nearer the time of registration the question of accidents and abuse should be brought up with the prospective minder. She should be asked to let the parent and social worker know if the child is injured while he is with her, and also to let both know if the child is in contact with any infectious disease, or is failing to eat or thrive in any way. It is more difficult for the minder to feel comfortable about letting the social worker know if the child arrives with bruising, burns, or what she suspects is non-accidental injury. It is therefore very important to routinely discuss this area with all prospective minders and let them know your department's policy about abusing parents, and the help that is available to parents who are having difficulties.

The other important area of understanding to establish is the relationship with the clinic and health visitor, and to be sure that the clinic knows when registration is completed and is informed about children who go to the minder. The minder should have a clear understanding with the parent about who takes the child for prophylaxes, progress checks, and dental treatment.

Working with registered minders

There is no statutory requirement of visiting to minders, but a wise department will suggest that minimum visiting to each registered minder would be quarterly for a review on: (a) the children being minded; (b) changes in the kind of care offered; (c) the training needs of the minder; (d) the fees they charge; (e) any difficulties with the natural parents over: (i) relationships; (ii) timing; (iii) food; (iv) money; (v) clothing; (vi) toys.

Child minders are likely to need considerable support if you want them to remain minders beyond their first or second minded child. It is at this early stage that the seeds of a good supporting relationship with the social worker can be crucial. Your knowledge of child development will be challenged. Don't be afraid to say you don't know, but do go away and find out and come back and share how you got the advice you then give. Brush up your knowledge, especially on play and stimulus, and think of ways in which the minder can allow the conflicts of care to be acknowledged (see Exercise 3 on p. 38).

Consider running a group for your minders. This combines the advantage of weekly contact, and up-to-date information about vacancies, with the opportunity to offer them training, support and additional play facilities at the same time. It may be possible to obtain a craft teacher from your adult education institute, or a short course can be offered on safety in the home (health education), library services, play with waste material (Pre-school Playgroup Association) or first aid (St John's Ambulance Brigade). It helps to have a crèche for such a group, with a play leader responsible together with the minders, on a rota basis, for the care of all the children.

What happens when minding goes wrong

Most departments are reluctant to prosecute minders and prefer a policy of positive encouragement, or counselling out. Many minders take on too many children because they are undercharging, or to meet their own emotional needs. Work with them, helping them to value themselves and the service they offer, can be very rewarding, and encouragement for them to notice the individual development of each child can often lessen the need to go over their registration numbers. Careful assessment of the reason for a minder persistently taking on too many children is necessary, and if undercharging is one of the causes, then tactful work with both the minder and the parents will be called for.

Where the care that a minder is giving is such as to cause concern for the children, initially this should be discussed with the minder herself. If the situation continues, then a visit to the parent should include: a clear statement of the cause of anxiety (confirmed in writing if the parent is resistant); the fact that this has been discussed with the minder, but no change effected; the offer of alternative placement; discussion of how soon action is likely to be taken by the parent or by the social worker; information, where appropriate, that a place of safety order may be sought.

A minder may be prosecuted and yet continue minding, and some authorities have minders who have been prosecuted many times. The usual result is a fine and withdrawal of registration, but that simply pushes the minding into the illegal twilight. It is for this reason that most authorities adopt a policy of working with minders who are unsuitable but determined to mind, as at least in this way their access to the children remains open.

Shared day care

In most authorities the shortage of day-care places means that the idea of shared care is regarded as nonsense on economic grounds, but there are an increasing number of advocates of this system (e.g. Tizard, Moss and Perry 1976). The child benefits by having the individual care of the minder, and the facilities of the centre to which the minder is linked. Family centres in which either minder or parent is welcome with the child, where they can leave the child for part of the day, or where the minded child can go when the minder is ill or on holiday, clearly should be among the development goals for each local autority. Above all they offer a mixture of care opportunities and thus are able to serve a wide range of parents. The traditional conflict between the professional and the mother figure is minimised and the amount of each kind of care can be geared to the individual child. Shared day care needs to be seen as an investment in the future, not as just compensatory for disadvantaged families.

Parents and day care

What factors need to be taken into consideration when parents sort out what kind of day care will best meet their child's needs and their own? If you understand about the parents' own background and early parenting experiences you will be able to grasp the likely areas of conflict and can assess whether these are likely to be more easily resolved in a one-to-one or in a one-to-establishment type of relationship. It is therefore helpful to ask the parent if he is willing to share information concerning his personal relationships, marriage and parental background. Many workers feel this is intrusive and that parents are entitled to receive the resources of day care without revealing any of their own histories. Despite this, I am aware from experience that when a full history has been taken initially, it is possible to do a much better job of matching day care and parent. I have seen the enormous benefit to some young and inexperienced parents of being linked with an experienced and motherly minder, who understood and was able to accept the reason for the aggressive manner and apparently off-hand care given to the child. Thoughtful and imaginative work with a minder, with family centre or day nursery staff, and parent, can prevent long-term emotional damage to the child, and may avoid eventual breakdown of the situation.

Pressure of work may mean that you can only undertake an assessment of the situation and offer little more, but that early picture of the child's situation may offer clues for difficult decision-making later in the child's life. It will certainly make it less likely that the child will receive a multitude of alternative carers.

What should be the minimum assessment contact for day care for an under 5?

See a parent and child together and observe their interaction, looking for the non-verbal as well as the verbal clues (see *Good enough parenting*, CCETSW Study 1, 1978, Chapter 6, non-accidental injury case example, by Gill Gorell Barnes, with excellent case history and notes).

If you have *any* doubts about the parent–child relationship, ask to visit them at home, see the other parent, and have contact with the health visitor. Keep in touch with the family until you are satisfied that you understand the parent–child relationship sufficiently to help minder or nursery staff work with it.

Anyone caring for someone else's child on a long-term basis needs to know:

The child's routine: stage of development including feedings, speech and toilet training; likes and dislikes of food and clothing; favourite toy and comforter; history, including details of health, separations and good and bad experiences.

The parents' wishes about, for example, haircutting, table manners and sweets; how the parents can be contacted in an emergency.

About the family home – does it have a garden, pets, is it shared? If so, with whom? What kind of accommodation is it?

Parents' expectations of day care vary, so you need to find out: why they want it, for how long and on how many days; what they think it will offer (a) them; (b) the child; what they can afford and how willing they are to pay; how the parent can be contacted when a place is available; how important their work is to them: (a) financially; (b) socially (remembering ethnic/cultural factors); (c) emotionally.

As an office is often not the most suitable place to interview a parent and child, some authorities are tackling this problem in different ways. Some invite parents who want day care to come to a family centre, a health centre, or a special 'drop-in' facility, where the parent and child can use play materials, meet other parents who are seeking day care, and meet minders who have vacancies, together with the children they are already minding. The health or family centre staff can sometimes be included in the assessment work where there are particular difficulties. The team spirit these shared activities generate can contribute to the overall day-care programme.

Check-list 3 – *Your own authority's under 5s day care practice – can it be improved?*

Policy
Do we have a co-ordinator for services to under 5s?
Does it cost the parent the same for a minder, day nursery or family centre?
Is nursery education available at our day nurseries?
Do we advertise the advantage of registration for minders?
Do we encourage parents to seek placement advice from a specialist working solely with under 5s' day care?
Assessment
Is an assessment of the parent–child relationship included in recording of the application?
Are home visits a part of any assessment where there is doubt about the care a child is receiving?
Is the child's play part of the assessment?
Nurseries and family centres
Do they have groups for parents to: (a) help in management; (b) raise funds; (c) share in activities; (d) learn together; (e) practise parent skills?
Are they open long enough to meet parental needs?
Are the children from mixed social/economic/cultural groups? Could the mix be improved? How?
Is the staffing ratio enough to give time for staff to form relationships with parents, to share information both ways? Are enough of the staff on duty early and late to allow for this?
How are field-workers seen by the staff? How do they see the staff? Has a field-worker ever run/participated in a course or group at the centre?
Can the centre undertake developmental measurement of children? Can it offer a programme for an individual child's development needs?
Is there a link with a residential establishment and some understanding about what happens if a child is not collected by a certain time? What time? Whose decision? Have the parents been told?

Minders
Are they valued? Does their position in case-loads allow this?
Have we specialist workers for minders? Are their case-loads realistic? Do they have time to build relationships with nurseries, crèches, child abuse workers, fostering section, health visitors? How could their access to these be improved?
Do our minders have all the items listed on pp. 30–31 ('what you should know about your own authority in relation to child minders')?
Is there anything the authority can do to increase the number of minders available?
Do we have a salaried minder scheme? Can it be extended?
Do any of our minders already link with, or could links be made with: (a) particular centres; (b) nursery schools; (c) adult education classes?
When did you last discuss, with a registered minder: (a) child development; (b) play; (c) toys; (d) hygiene; (e) safety; (f) money – or their charges?

Exercises

Role plays

1. On a very rainy day, Mrs Wright and Susan (aged 3) have come by appointment to apply for a day nursery place. Mrs Wright is married, and her husband works shifts. They live in rented accommodation and if Mrs Wright returns to her work as a computer operator they will be able to get a mortgage to buy a house. Susan is crying and demanding attention.
   Role play (a) an interview in a small office between Mrs Wright and the social worker, with a few toys for Susan to play with; (b) a group of a social worker, a social work assistant/play leader/volunteer, two minders, two other day-care applicants and three children. All play with the children and share what they are there for. Susan is cared for flexibly within this group situation and all members of the group can overhear and join in the interview between the social worker and Mrs Wright.
   Afterwards, discuss (i) which interview allowed more of the things the alternative carer will want to know to be revealed (including the child's development); (ii) ways in which the strengths of each could be combined.

2. Mrs Charles, a West Indian, lives on the top floor of a multi-occupied house and wants to be a daily minder. She has three rooms and a kitchen and shares a W/C and bathroom one flight downstairs. She has four children. The two older ones are in the West Indies with their maternal grandmother, Clive (aged 6) is at school and Annette (aged 3) is at home. Mr Charles works for public transport. Mrs Charles has an old injury to her left arm, which makes it difficult for her to find employment.
   Role play a child-minding-specialist worker's first visit to the home.
   Afterwards, discuss (i) whether you would expect to be able to register her, and on what conditions; (ii) which areas you would expect to have to work on before registration was complete, or in refusing registration; (iii) if registration is refused, what alternatives you would offer her; (iv) what suggestions you would make for involving her in day care for under 5s.

3. Maisie Carr, experienced minder of five years' standing, is having acute difficulties with Donna (aged 2) and her food. Donna's mother, Shirley Sims, allows Donna to eat whenever she wants, including late in the evening. Donna is overweight and whines or cries if she is not given food whenever she asks.

Role play an interview between Maisie Carr and her social worker.

Try letting Maisie practise what to do or say by suggesting that she pretend a chair is Shirley and telling it what she *really* thinks and feels about the food problem. Then try the social worker pretending to be Shirley and let Maisie rehearse how to explain the problem. If these go well, ask Maisie to pretend she is Shirley, having heard what Maisie said about the problem.

Afterwards, discuss (i) practical advice you would offer; (ii) at what stage the worker should offer to see Shirley.

Allocations

The following are deliberately brief outlines, for this is the kind of information synopsis on which a lot of allocations of day nursery placements have to be made in practice.

Tasks

1. Your first task is to decide, in each case, which would be the best day care from the full range available in your authority. (If this is not known, say that it consists of day nurseries, family centres, salaried minders, minders, 1 o'clock clubs daily, a group for mother and minders and children once a week, a playbus once a week, a mother and toddler club twice a week, daily play-groups for children aged 2½ years or over, and a nursery school for children over 3 years, both of which only offer half-day placements.)

(a) Non-English-speaking Indian mother of 3½-year-old girl is deserted by her husband and is offered a job in her brother's business. Her 6-year-old son comes out of school at 3.15 p.m. Mother requests a nursery place.

(b) Single West Indian father has custody of his 18-month-old daughter. He is a member of a touring acting company. His mother and sisters live nearby and share in the evening care of the child. He requests a nursery place.

(c) Depressed mother, who is not working but has good earning potential in a 9–5 job, is married to a gambler, who works shifts. There are multiple financial problems. The two children are 2½ and a 5½-year-old, who comes out of school at 3.30 p.m. Request is for day care – unspecified.

(d) Two working parents have had a minder for their 2-year-old. The minder has moved out of the district. There were endless problems of rivalry between mother and minder and child, who has now had three minders. Request is for a nursery.

(e) An 18-year-old, white, single mother lives in a council flat with her half-caste daughter of 6 months. She has a very difficult journey to visit her own mother. The child has been left unattended for up to an hour on two occasions. The father of the child is not known. Mother requests a nursery place so she can go to work but she has never been employed. She draws supplementary benefit.

(f) A 36-year-old divorced, schizoid mother, who has only had one hospitalisation, but whose employment is spasmodic and yields a low wage, has a 2-year-old. Mother's mood swings are acute and she is currently behaving in a fairly bizarre way. The child sees his father and stepmother at weekends. He was previously in a private nursery, but finance is no longer available for this. Mother is on supplementary benefit and requests day care – unspecified.

(g) A 3½-year-old Chinese boy, who speaks no English, is often left with his brother of 9 and no other adult. He has twice caused a fire. Both parents work until 6 p.m. Previously an aunt lived with the family, then there were the summer holidays; now they request day care – unspecified.

2. Your second task is to allocate places when you only have the following full-time care places available: (a) one place in a family centre; (b) one place in a day nursery; (c) one place with a salaried minder who minds three – others are 4 years and 6 months old; (d) one place with an elderly minder who already has one other child and is only registered for two.

What advice would you offer those to whom you cannot offer the ideal solution or any full care?

4 Into Care

There are two basic routes by which a child comes into the care of the local authority. He may be received into care, under Section 2 of the Child Care Act 1980, (CCA 1980) if he is lost or abandoned, or at the request of his parents, any responsible adult or the police. Alternatively, a court may commit a child to the local authority's care. It is not the aim of this book to cover the various forms of legislation under which a child may be committed to care, although Table 4.1 shows the possible legal routes.

Of the 100,200 children in care in England and Wales in 1980, 44,300 were in care under the 1948 Children Act (which was replaced in 1980 by the Child Care Act), while 47,700 were the subject of care orders made in the juvenile court. Some 6,000 were the subject of care orders from other courts (Department of Health and Social Security 1982).

These figures are of those actually in care on 31 March 1980. Beside them consider that 41,900 came into care and 40,100 left care during that one year. Of those leaving care 17,000 had been in care under eight weeks which underlines the importance of short-term care being well handled, and the need for preventive measures to be extended even further. Some 4,400 children had been in care between eight weeks and six months, while for another 2,000 their time in care had lasted between six months and a year. The remaining three statistical periods should give you cause for grave concern, stressing the need for clear goals for children in long-term care, as outlined in Chapter 5. There were 6,800 children who had been in care between one and three years, 4,800 between three and five years, and 5,200 had been more than five years in care when they left it (Department of Health and Social Security 1980). For these children I wonder what goals had been formulated, what purpose they saw in their long time in public care, and what role their parents or families had been able to fulfil in their lives.

The fundamental difference between a child who is committed to care and the one who has come into care under Section 2 lies in the rights of the parents (see Chapter 5, p. 63–5, regarding the taking of parental rights and duties). In committing a child to care the court is saying that the local authority will then decide where and with whom the child will live, go to school, and what medical care the child will receive. The only remaining parental right is to request

Table 4.1 Routes into care

CHILD CARE ACT 1980
Section 2 Voluntary reception into care

Section 57(b) Closure of a voluntary home – only applies if child appears to be over 17 years

CHILDREN AND YOUNG PERSONS ACT 1969
Section 28(1) Place of safety order

Section 20(1) Interim order

Section 1(3) Care order following proceedings in which Section 1(2) (a)–(f) have been proved, and the need for an order also shown

Section 7(7) Care order following proceedings where the child has been found guilty of an offence punishable by imprisonment if committed by an adult

Section 29(3) Detention in care at the request of the police, pending a court appearance within 72 hours

Section 23(1) Remand

FAMILY LAW REFORM ACT 1969
Section 7(2) & (3) Wardship proceedings in the High Court. Care order but the court continues to exercise jurisdiction

MATRIMONIAL CAUSES ACT 1973
Section 43(1) Divorce proceedings in a county or High Court – care order

DOMESTIC PROCEEDINGS AND MAGISTRATES COURTS ACT 1978
Section 89 Divorce proceedings in a magistrates court – care order

FOSTER CHILDREN ACT 1980
Section 12 Removal from a private foster home on a place of safety order. Section 12(5) applies if child appears to be over 17 years

ADOPTION ACT 1958
Section 43(3) Removal from an adoptive home (to be Section 34 of Adoption Act 1976 when implemented) – care order

CHILDREN ACT 1975
Section 17(1) (b) Refusal of an adoption order – care order.

Section 36(3) (when implemented). Revocation of a custody order – care order

GUARDIANSHIP ACT 1973
Section 2(2) (b) Refusal of a guardianship order – care order

the faith that the child be brought up in. The parent also retains the duty to pay for the upkeep of his child until he is 16, even though the local authority may refuse permission for the parent to see the child.

First considerations

When their child comes into care there is a loss of privacy for the parents. The information that you sought in your assessment will be shared more widely, whether the child is committed or you are receiving him into care. If the child has been the subject of care proceedings it is likely that a lot of information will have been made available to the court, but this will omit the more personal details about both the child and his parents that a future carer will need.

The knowledge that a child will want about his parents, if, for instance, they should be killed, may be very different from the statement you have prepared for a court to show that a care order is needed. It can be very difficult to obtain the parents' co-operation in gaining this more intimate information during the first few weeks of care following court proceedings, for it can aggravate the sense of loss the parents feel, if they are asked to supply such details. Where it seems likely that a child may be committed to care, either try to obtain this type of information early in your contact, or add the need for it to the plan of action you negotiate with the family. It helps to give the family a written plan of what the authority intends to do as soon as possible after the hearing. In this you could stress the child's need for information about his parents and show the family it is something that they can do with and for a child that the local authority is unable to do.

If the child has to come into care as part of crisis arrangements, then your pattern will be different and for this there is an additional check-list at the end of the chapter (check-list 5). Try to remember to delegate and share the arrangements as much as possible, and not to allow yourself to get caught into the child or family's sense of panic.

The forms that the local authority require to be completed at the point of reception into care often feel like bureaucratic intrusion at a point of painful crisis. Try to become really familiar not just with their format, but also with the reasons for each question before you actually have to use them. You should expect the parent to ask *why* you need to know his National Insurance number and the place of marriage, and to be comfortable yourself with the reasons. It is good practice to complete the same forms, particularly the one giving the child's medical history, in respect of a child committed to care, although not all authorities suggest this. It ensures that information is available in a standard form for every child in care.

Medical

Any child coming into care should be examined by a doctor. A freedom from infection certificate (FFI) is usually obtained. Ask the doctor to check particularly for lice, scabies and impetigo as these can get overlooked if the doctor's focus is on infectious diseases like chickenpox or measles. Remember, as you decide 'not to bother about an FFI this time', that you could be introducing infection to a children's home, where it could persist for a year or more, or to a foster home that may well cease to foster as a result of that additional burden you have imposed, not to mention the unpleasant health hazards to which you may expose a number of people completely unnecessarily.

Placement: basic principles

Wherever possible you should arrange for a child and his parents to go on a visit to his placement before he comes into care. (The obvious exception to the possibility for this is where a youngster is committed for an assessment by the court.) Local authorities use several different forms of care for children, but overall is the requirement in law that the child be given the care that is best for his welfare and in accordance with his wishes, if he is able to express them. This is not to conflict with the interests of the community (Child Care Act 1980, Section 18).

Where the expectation is that the child will be in care for a short term, then it is particularly important that he go beforehand to visit the placement with a parent if at all possible. Encourage the parent to become familiar with the environment into which the child will go and to get to know the people who will be caring for the child. This lessens the stress on both child and parent at the time of reception into care, and increases the probability of the child returning home.

The first choice of placement that has to be considered by the local authority is with relatives or friends of the parents, as mentioned in Chapter 2, but the next is that the child be placed with foster parents (Child Care Act 1980, Section 21 (1)(a)). In 1980 38,400 of the children in care were in foster homes and the numbers of those fostered have shown an increase over the last few years

(Office of Population Censuses and Surveys 1982).

Other placements that are likely at the point of entry to care are in assessment homes, although increasing use is being made of day assessment. This enables the child to remain at home, attend a day centre, and participate in school and other activities while his behaviour is monitored. His parents may also be involved for part of the time, either attending in the evening, or, if available, for group sessions during the day. The child has plenty of time to explain to those around him what is important to him, what problems he sees himself as having and what he thinks he is good at. He will also be assessed by an educational psychologist and a psychiatrist. Where the assessment is undertaken in a residential setting, similar work may be done with the child, but here we find less parental involvement and the additional complications of the effect of institutionalisation on the child.

At the end of a period that may vary from three to six weeks, a decision will be reached about his future placement. Ideally the child himself should be involved in this decision, bearing in mind his possibly limited capacity to understand what kind of placement is available and that his opinion is likely to have been coloured by what he has heard from other children. I have suggested a way in which he could be involved in the next chapter under the heading 'Placement'.

The decision that a child should come into care is not one that a fieldworker should make alone. It is normally a departmental requirement that a senior take the decision, but even where it is not, it is good practice to check one's own view of the case with a colleague and, where possible, involve a residential worker also. It is easy to fall into the parents' view of what is, or is not, possible to arrange as alternative care, rather than challenging their assumptions. They are often not aware of the damage that even a short period of institutional care can (but need not) do to their child, and to their relationship with him.

Confirm the arrangements in writing to the parents, including the details of time and date, of how and when visiting can happen, by whom and on whose 'say so'. In some children's homes it is not convenient for parents to visit at mealtimes; in others this is encouraged, and a lot of work is done with the parents over the meal tables as part of sharing care. In some foster homes there may be days on which it would be difficult to include a natural parent, or there may be problems about visits when the children have just got in from school. Parents on night duty may have a quite different perception of times, so it is helpful to sort out with them when they would expect to visit and at what time they would think it reasonable to do so. Bear in mind, for example, that bedtimes for 7-year-olds vary considerably!

When you are feeling harassed and anxious about the arrangements for reception into care, it is difficult to remember that the parents and child will want answers to basic questions about the place to which the child will be going. Try to prepare a list of the kinds of questions to which you would want answers for them, or, if there is time, do a list with the child, so that you are ready to ask any foster parent or establishment that you may be making arrangements with. It can be a good group exercise. Some of the questions that the child may ask are: Who will look after me? What will I call them? Who will meet me today? Who will share my bedroom? Will they turn all the lights out at night? What time is bedtime (check for each age)? What happens if I wet the bed? Can I take my teddy, my poster, my continental quilt? Do I have to eat everything they give me? Will they know I *hate* eggs/can't eat pork? How many children are there? What ages? Will they all go to school during the day? Will I? Which school? What about uniform? Do I have to wear their clothes? What time will I have to get up? Can Mum and Dad come and see me? Can my friends? When? How often? Will I get any pocket-money? How much (check ages)? Can I smoke? Can I go out? Can I go home? How long does it take to get there?

Admission

At the time of admission, the child needs a 'bridge' person, someone who will help him to get his things ready at home, and stays with him in the new situation until bedtime. If he is going to a foster home perhaps the foster mother would come with you to collect the child, or one of the foster family, or maybe a residential worker from the children's home, if that is where the child is going. If neither the residential worker nor the foster mother is able to come with you, try to involve a member of the child's family, a friend of the parents, or a family aide.

The concept of the 'bridge' person has gained some ground in practice with younger children, but unfortunately it has not been so generally recognised with older children, where the appropriate person could be a child from the establishment to which the child is being admitted.

In arranging the admission to care it is important to establish with those receiving the child who will actually be meeting you at the door and showing you around. The aim is usually that the same person will put a new child to bed as will get him up the following morning. Continuity of care is recognised as important, but staff shifts make for some complications.

One enterprising London Borough started a system of the admitting fieldworker writing a letter addressed to the child, describing the events of the day on which they came into care. This could be done equally well by the 'bridge' person, or by a residential worker, who has been to the child's home, or the child could be encouraged to do this himself. The letter needs to include details about personal belongings and family pets, and to acknowledge any difficulties and rows. It can also include future plans.

Wherever the child is placed, in foster home, community home, reception home or remand, the feelings of the child, parents, field-workers and residential social workers are likely to be similar, whether the child is subject to a care order or has been received into care. The intensity of feelings may vary in each case, but you will find that *some* degreee of most of the following types of feeling will play their part. The list is intended to prompt you in your thinking about the cases you are working with. It could also form the basis for a group discussion about the impact of care on those involved. It is based on one compiled in 1981 by Sue Allen and Gill Munrow, two students at Bedford College, University of London, to whom my thanks are due.

Transfer of care – its emotional impact on those involved

Feelings of the child

Anger: Towards parents, towards new authority figures. 'Why me?'

Confusion: About the length of time and the reason he is in care, the distance he is from home, the structure of the children's home, the rules of the foster home.

Disorientation: The need to fit into many different roles, to conform to different and unknown standards.

Guilt: 'I've been put away'; fantasies about punishment, which may be linked to parents having threatened him with just that in the past. 'Have I done something wrong? Why does going away make it better? If I do it again, will I be sent away from here?'

Insecurity: 'Are my parents/siblings/friends OK? What happens if I am sick, wet the bed? Make a mess? Tear my clothes? Is it really safe here? Who will come and visit me? What will be different? What can I take with me from home?'

Loss: Of parents, home, siblings, school, friends, social life, privacy. Need to grieve, space to cry; place and person to talk to about loss.

Pain: Complexity and intensity of many unfamiliar feelings may be overwhelming and need a great deal of sensitivity to sort them out.

Stress: Memories of the crisis/trauma which led to reception or committal to care may limit the capacity to respond to care situation and adaptive skills may be diminished.

Threat to identity: Admission to an institution or incorporation into a warm and dominant foster family may lead to a subsequent lack of trust in self and others.

Excitement and curiosity may cover many of these and help with the level of pain. Relief from stress may make the other elements diminish. In each case use these positives with the child while giving the opportunity for the other feelings to emerge gradually through play or quiet talking time.

Feelings of the parents

Anger: Towards the court or social services department or voluntary body involved in care proceedings. Why are they doing this?

Towards the child, for needing to be received into care, exposing the parents' lack of resources/friends/capacity to control.

At bureaucracy and its inadequacies and demands (forms, no ideal care solutions, etc.).

Anxiety: What are our legal rights? Will we get our child back? What will it be like for him? What happens if he is ill? Unhappy?

Exposed: Details of family relationships and way of life have been written down and given to strangers. 'Will the neighbours get to know about the reason he is in care? Will it be in the papers?'

Guilt: Breaking the biological tie – 'Our child cared for by someone else – are we bad parents?' Self-recrimination – 'If only we'd . . .'

Inadequacy: Having to ask for help.

Pain: The separation and loss; our child becoming, even for a short while, someone else's to care for.

Relief: The problem of the care of our child is solved; someone else can take the responsibility/tackle the problem.

Robbed: Of our role with our child, of our status as parents, of our intimate language with our child.

Unresolved conflicts: The repetition of their own childhood rejections by their parents; exposure of conflicts between parents.

Feelings of the field social worker

Anxiety: Is the timing right for the child's needs? Will the child benefit as hoped? Go home as planned? Has my assessment been accurate?

Compromise: Between what is ideal for the child and what is possible in reality.

Conflict: Between parents' values, my own values, those of society and those of the agency.

Failure: Inability to keep the family together or find a solution outside care.

Pain: The whole process of reception or committal is sad and depressing and needs to be faced with courage and honesty.

Relief: The problem is temporarily solved, especially where it is in a case of a crisis or where the child has been at risk, the subject of your being nagged by other agencies, or of frequent referrals. The child is 'safe'.

Self-preservation: What if I had done nothing and something had gone wrong?

Feelings of those receiving the child (foster parents, residential staff, etc.)

Affection: Wanting to give the child a caring experience.

Ambivalence: The newcomer's unfamiliarity can be unsettling as it can highlight alternative ways of doing things, or disrupt.

Anger: At parents, when a child has been ill-treated or is behind in development.

   At parents or social worker, when child is brought at an inconvenient time of day/night.

Determination: That the child will conform to their way of life – 'that's how things are here'; 'Now you're here you'll have to . . . '

Guilt: Taking the child, in some measure, from the parents.

Injustice: 'Who's left holding the baby?'

Resentment: That parents can give up their child.

Worthiness: Feeling that they help parents who can't manage, the child who needs care and, maybe, that they are 'better' than the parents who have given up their child.

Feelings of other children in the same placement
Anxiety: Will the newcomer upset the way things are?
Insecurity: Each new arrival/departure reminds each child of his personal uncertainty, upsets the balance of relationships within the home.
Jealousy: Guarding of friends, privileges, chairs, toys. The newcomer may be exploited for his 'greenness' or scapegoated as the cause of lost group cohesion.

In each case that you deal with, try running through the list to think out your way of working with the child and his family. You will think of more feelings involved than those included in the list, but it is intended to help you focus on the feelings that are involved for each child for whom you arrange a placement.

Children of all ages need to be allowed ways in which they can express their feelings about the transfer of care that has taken place. Young ones can be helped to play out the loss they experience by using dolls to ask the questions about their families that they want to ask. For older ones, offer writing and drawing materials and, above all, space and time. With their peers they may need the brave denial, but on their own be glad to admit the fears and apprehensions they are experiencing. Be careful that such 'fronts' are not subsequently demolished by your use of your 'inside' knowledge.

Short- and long-term care

If the child has come into care short term, then a clear contract about length of care needs to be established. As soon as this is breached, for whatever reason, then a new understanding of the purpose of the child being in care needs to be established. The role of the short-term caretaker, who expects the child to return home, is very different from that of a person working towards a future long-term placement either in another children's home, or a permanent substitute home. A 'story book', started at the time of the change in duration of care, can be the focus for some different work. For example:

John Brown went to live with Mary and Peter Smith and their three children, Diana, Sharon and Mark, when his mother, Alice Brown, went into a psychiatric hospital on 17 September 1981. John's father, Ben Lewis, had left home three months before and no one knew where he was living. In hospital, the doctors found that Alice needed more treatment than they had expected and so John had to stay longer with Mary and Peter than the three weeks he had expected to be there. John started going to school with Mark. He liked Woodfield School and quickly made friends with Simon Lester. He went with Mary to visit his mother in the hospital. She was in Summers Ward and the hospital was called Pembury Downs.

The book may then be kept up by the foster parents or residential staff in preparation for John's future. It could have parts added to it by the child's parents.

The field-work task is to ensure that all parties understand the reason for the change in plan, and to establish for how long the new situation can be maintained. For how long is that short-term foster home the appropriate placement? For how long can the children's home be regarded as the right place for him? Do not collude with the parent in thinking that the extension of care is 'only another week' but look at the implications for the child of that extension, and test its realism for the future.

Help a child leaving home for long-term care to look not only at the good of what he is gaining and the bad of what he is leaving behind, but also at what he will miss from home, and the difficulties that lie ahead. Your own inclination may be to paint a rosy picture of the future, that all will be enjoyable. Try to keep the balance, and to value what has been important to the child in the life he is leaving. With an older child you can ask him what he will miss most, and what he will be glad to leave.

I recently moved an ESN lad of 16 from his long-stay foster home to a residential trade training school. We did two sets of charts together, 'What I will miss' and 'Who I will miss'. We talked about why, and in what order of priority. It formed a focus for him to say what the cost of the move would be, and on arrival gave him a written beginning to communicating about his home life with the residential staff.

Where a child has only been a short while in the first care situation it is tempting to move him on without full thought about the double loss he is thus experiencing. Many of the feelings that were involved in the original admission will re-emerge and need time and space to be sorted out. New fears about loss of identity will be strong, for the child is then twice removed from home. Parental involvement and understanding at this point of transfer can be crucial. It is at this time that the emotional 'space' that the child filled in the home situation is likely to begin to close over, particularly if it takes place at the end of the first two or three months of care, the time at which the child's family identity is suffering its most acute crisis. A conscious decision should therefore be reached as to whether the home situation is intended to fade out of the child's life; that is, whether you are really seeking to terminate parental contact.

If the child is not going to spend the remainder of his childhood functioning outside the family, what routes back into the family are being clearly established at the point of decision for longer term care?

In planning for a child to come into care it is easy to allow the practical needs and problems to cloud the emotional ones. Make sure you give your clients and yourself time. Even in crises it is possible to ensure that 'rushing back to the office' does not panic you into leaving a child before he has attached himself to someone in the new environment. In particular, aim to change policy in your department so that admission to care is given the time and personnel, the 'bridge' person and the transport, that such a financially and emotionally expensive undertaking warrants.

Check-list 4 – *Reception into care*

Have I...
Completed the forms and had them authorised?
Got an FFI?
Got a history of both parents for the child to have an adequate picture of them if they disappeared or were killed?
Got names of the parents' next of kin or friends, who could give the child some personal knowledge of his parents if an accident occurred?
Recorded the child's nickname, feeding habits, likes and dislikes, friends, toys, or special belongings, fantasies, night-time routine?
Checked that: (a) the child has enough clothing for the placement arranged; (b) the placement has all the equipment it needs to take this child?
Arranged when and how the 'bridge' person will arrive at the child's home?
Got equipment for the journey – Tissues, nappies, potty, sweets to suck to prevent travel sickness, bowl for sick child?
Have the following been arranged to go with the child?
One change of clothing, more if possible; night-time comforter, toys, picture of parent if available; special feeding things, e.g. bottle, feeding cup, spoon, mug; special belongings, e.g. records, posters.
Have the following been given to the parent?
Name and address and telephone number of the placement and who to make arrangements with;

As many details as possible about the placement.

When and how you will give them news of their child?

Name, address and telephone number of the social worker who will be responsible for their child while he is in care, with an explanation if that worker is not you.

Have the following been written out to give the foster mother or establishment:

Parents' whereabouts at different times of the day, and how to contact them?

Details of the reason for admission to care and the legal grounds under which the child is in care and their implications?

A copy of the recorded details about the child's nickname, etc.?

Details of the child's medical history and the name and address of his GP?

Details of the child's school, whether he is to go to school while in care, and if so who to contact at his school for up-to-date details of the child's level of attainment?

Who will pay for what clothing and how and when?

Any other financial arrangements special to the placement?

Who may visit; who may take the child out and for how long; who may discharge the child from care and what to do if suddenly presented with a request for this?

Social worker's name, office address, telephone number and the emergency telephone number if a standby service is offered?

Check-list 5 – *Crisis reception into care*

1. Before racing around arranging placement, check whether the family is known to other agencies: (a) the health visitor; (b) education welfare; (c) medical social workers; (d) Family Welfare Association or Family Service Units; (e) schools;

and THINK what strengths they can offer: (a) information? (b) Sharing the crisis with the children? (c) Being a 'bridge' person? (d) Arranging overnight care?

2. Stop and plan what to leave out of your normal reception into care routine, bearing in mind:

(a) Do you have to do everything personally? Could a volunteer, home help, social work assistant, family aide, or clerk do some of the tasks? E.g. seek a placement? Take the child for an FFI? Write out details of the placement for parents?

(b) Time and distance factors and their impact on children.

(c) The local authorities' requirements – this will affect what you are *allowed* to leave out!

(d) Transport arrangements.

(e) What you *can* do afterwards – LIST it or it will be forgotten!

3. REMEMBER to give the children time to: (a) cry; (b) ask; (c) remember; (d) settle into the placement.

4. ENSURE that parents know where their children are, with the telephone number, address and visiting arrangements, as soon as possible after the reception into care. If the children of a family have to be separated, ENSURE that *each* child, as well as the adults concerned, has a written copy of where each of his siblings is placed.

Exercise in prevention and reception into care

The O'Connor Family

Mary and James O'Connor have two children, Debbie (aged 3) and Mark (aged 6½). They live in a two-bedroom council flat in an inner London Borough. They moved there a year after Mark's birth, having been homeless for six months and in bed and breakfast accommodation.

Mary is expecting another baby in a month's time. Since Debbie was born, Mary's mother has died. James's mother lives in Liverpool and has only met the children twice, the last time being earlier this year. Mary and her mother-in-law have never got on well. All other O'Connor relatives live either in Ireland or Liverpool and are not in contact with the family. Mary has a sister in Ireland with whom she is close and to whom she writes. The sister has been over to stay with the family several times.

James has had all his holiday entitlement from work and has been told if he has more time off work he'll lose his job. He works shifts, 7–3, 3–11 and 11–7, and earns a low net wage. The family budget reasonably and there are no debts, but neither are there any savings. Mark had difficulty settling into school but now enjoys it. Debbie goes to play-group three times a week.

The family have requested reception into care for the two children for the coming confinement; Mary has to be in hospital for ten days as there were difficulties at Debbie's birth.

The area team's Section 1 budget has only £25 left for the next six weeks. There is a local foster mother who would have a vacancy to offer at the relevant time. She is the same age as James's mother, and has a 14-year-old son, Matthew, living at home. There is a vacancy in a children's home about twenty minutes' walk away from the flat.

Tasks

1. Decide what preventive work to try, and list; (a) various actions you would need to take; (b) considerations involved in implementing your plan.

2. One week before the confinement. Your preventive plans have failed. Plan reception into care: (a) with placement at the foster mother's home; (b) with placement in the children's home, as the foster mother took an emergency admission last week, when you thought Mary's sister was coming over from Ireland.

   List in each case: (i) what actions you would take; (ii) what actions one of the parents needs to take; (iii) how you will arrange the admission.

5 Children in Care

Placement

Any child in residential care should be offered what Winnicott (1965) calls 'real experiences of good care, comfort and control'. Good care is defined as including 'a sense of timing that can allow personal experiences to be completed and a sense of achievement attained . . . a recognition of each child's needs and an attempt to meet them with a feeling response'. For children in establishments the conflict lies between individual needs and compliance to group pressures. Despite the increase in fostering, the majority of children in care are in community homes. About 6,000 of those in care in 1977 were living in community homes with education on the premises, while more than 9,500 of the remainder were in homes catering for more than twelve children.

In these large group situations, individual needs are difficult to meet. Children's homes can be encouraged to individualise their care of each child by:

1. *Operating a system of 'specials'* where each member of staff takes a particular responsibility for a few children. The 'special' liaises with school and home and with the fieldworker concerned. She takes responsibility for the personal care of the child, the day-to-day decisions, his clothing and medical supervision.

2. *Defining the particular needs within the group of children* and organising the staff structure to meet the need. This involves looking at what additional staff resources, not manpower, may be required. For example, in a home with a number of children who are unsure or uncomfortable about touch, or who crave physical affection and seek it inappropriately, the staff, having defined the need, might arrange their duty rota to allow extra staff time at bedtime and getting up, with a view to making natural touch opportunities more readily available. Alongside this they would set up a staff support group, to share and discuss appropriate physical handling of the children and the emotional conflicts this can arouse.

3. *Involving the parent, fieldworker or other significant adults* in the child's life, in the care offered, and defining with each the particular role they are undertaking. If the child has become

separated from his own culture by virtue of his placement and yet wishes to retain his cultural identity, then the home should seek to clarify who will help the child reinforce that identity and in what ways. Posters, books, toys, music, food and clothing can all play an important part in valuing a child's personal and cultural heritage.

Choosing a placement for a child is a heavy responsibility. Often it is dependent on where a vacancy is available rather than real selection, yet where recommendations of assessment centres have been followed through it has been shown that the placement has a greater chance of success (Reinach and Roberts 1979). A child's needs should be defined and recorded and this should include a note of his own wishes (Child Care Act 1980, Section 18).

One way of discussing placement possibilities with a youngster is to take certain basic elements of caring for a child and establish which are the most important to him. You can compile your own list, but Table 5.1 may help you start.

Table 5.1

Love	*Control*	*Participation*
Encouragement	Boundaries/Limits/Routine	Activities/Hobbies
Love	Dependence/Independence	Companionship
Parent figures	Involvement in decisions	Education
Relationship with adults	Privacy	Fun
Security/Continuity	Respect/Individuality	Holidays
Touch/Physical contact	Responsibility	
	Trust/Dependability	

	The physical	*His identity*
	Clothing	Knowledge of own history
	Food	Knowledge of own parents
	Money	Knowledge of own siblings
	Roof	Knowledge of own culture
	Space	Religion
	Warmth	Roots

I have grouped the elements in areas that I consider have natural links, but you may find other combinations work better for you. If he is able, let the child select his own ten areas of most importance. Next, ask the child to say what would be really good and what bad in those areas that are important to him. I think an example may make it clearer.

Table 5.2 is a chart I did with an 11-year-old girl, a half-caste,

Table 5.2 Placements

Basic element of care	Good	+					−				Bad
		4	3	2	1	0	1	2	3	4	
Roots	Local shops available		X				ø				Away in the country, no shops
Responsibility	To be trusted			X	*		ø				To be watched
Respect	Have a say in how things are done			X	*		ø				To be told
Education	Go to *my* school	X			*		ø				Go to a new school
Companionship	Still have my mates	X	*				ø				To be no one there I know
Cultural links	Some other black children			X	*		ø				To be the only black child
Food	Hamburgers and curry		X							ø*	Salad
Warmth	Good heating	X					*	ø			No heating
Space	Not to have to sleep alone	*ø								X	Own room
Clothing	Play clothes – not 'posh'			X			*			ø	Have to wear a uniform

Notes

X is where her present placement came, according to the child concerned

ø is where I think she would have put her new placement at the time of her move

* is where I think she would have put her new placement two months after starting there

Some of the amelioration is due to the 'bad' having less importance once she was accepted by her new peer group and settled to new routines.

who had to move to a new residential home because of behaviour problems. Together we selected the areas that were important to her; alongside these we put her good and bad extremes. The order of the elements is her choice of importance. It is important to let the child give you the extremes of good and bad. I would certainly not have thought of salad as the opposite of hamburgers and curry!

Having listed the good and bad we marked her present placement on the chart (X). When we had been together to visit the placement I discussed it with her in the light of the chart. Sadly I didn't get her to fill it in, but have given my impression of what she said at that time (Ø). Similarly, after she had been there two months we compared again (*).

What was demonstrated by this method were the necessary areas of work for me to undertake with the child. Aware of the gaps and contrasts, these formed a focus for discussion about why her ideal could not be met, and some confrontation regarding her own responsibility in this. I included in my contact with her visits to shops and outings for hamburgers and curry, but also helped her to maintain contact with her former school friends and a West Indian housemother from her previous placement. These offset her feelings of loss of companions and cultural links.

The areas she chose within the elements of care are very simple, but the omission from the basic list also told me a lot. There was, for example, no element chosen from the Love group and only roots and culture from her identity group. This was a good reflection of the poverty of this child's experience, despite some excellent and caring residential work with her.

Alongside the question of choice of placement, you need knowledge of the establishments available to you. The role of children's homes is under critical survey at present. Those involved in Intermediate Treatment are seeking to demonstrate that delinquent youngsters should not be placed in community homes with education. Certainly the theory that 'at least they are catching up on their schooling' has been shown to be fallacious by the report on community homes, which highlighted the lack of skilled teaching staff available, and the low level of educational attainment in CH(E)s (Department of Education and Science 1980).

The difficulties of placing a newly received adolescent into care with a family are equally daunting. An adolescent needs to struggle against boundaries and limits with familiar adults, to find his own identity. To remove all the known boundaries, substitute new family norms and expect him to conform and grow to independence, while the foster family tends to encourage dependency, is setting a high goal for him. The foster family are likely to find the situation far from rewarding. Where a lot of support has been offered to both the foster families and the youngster, for example in the Kent Project (Hazel 1981), there has been success in this kind of placement, but there are few foster parents able to undertake this very demanding task.

I would commend to you Lothian region's policy, that is, that no child should remain in public care for more than two years. By this they mean that every child, by the time they have been in care two years, should either be in the process of returning to their own family or have been offered a permanent substitute family. Children's homes are to be used, in the main, as places for interim work and treatment.

In implementing this policy, Lothian have had to make some difficult choices, focusing on those under 11, where the statistical likelihood of successful placement in families is significantly higher. The Lothian policy has been made explicit to the older children in their care and work with them has been aimed towards supplementing institutional care rather than seeking permanent families.

To carry out their plan, Lothian have had to look very carefully at the decisions reached on the children in their care. The natural parent's role in the child's life is closely examined. Plans of work with the parent are given time contracts and the parent is faced, early in the care period, with the reality that his/her child needs permanent and stable care in a family situation. If the child's natural family are unable to supply this, then an alternative and permanent family is sought. The legal problems of such a policy are, of course, considerable, but it is the emotional difficulties that usually cause hesitation in implementing it. Most of us are reluctant to sever the links that may exist with a natural family. Although it has been shown that for a child who has been in care over a year and had infrequent contact with his parents during that period, there is little likelihood of his returning home, it must be remembered that to that child, his parents may still be the most significant people in his life (Lasson 1978).

Defining roles and parental involvement

Try clarifying your policy with a family by using the list of basic elements of care to establish from whom the child is receiving each element. From whom does he receive encouragement, love, etc.? Whose limits does he respect? The residential worker's? The council's? His parents'? Where is the focus of his participation? Is it at home or in care? Where your answers show that the child's needs are being met largely from the 'in care' situation, then you should be helping the parents to see how they can increase their role, so that 'in care' is a real partnership of parents and carers.

Remember that visiting a foster home or establishment can be a daunting and threatening experience for parents. Offer them the chance to criticise and make suggestions about the care their child is receiving. Support them in effecting appropriate changes for their child, to meet his individual needs. Assist them to identify what is being gained by the 'in care' situation. Facilitate their contact with their child by offering fares or transport, or by taking them to visit if going on their own is too difficult.

The alternative to involving the parents more is to help them to surrender their child permanently. The challenge to you is to insist that those are the only two options. Little family contact, with the children's hopes being endlessly dashed, is not an available choice.

The residential worker's task, or the foster parent's, is to clarify similarly with the child that a new life out of his own family situation is being built and to check with the child that this is what he wants to do. It is so much easier to dodge this issue, particularly if the child is in a foster home, but defining why John remains in care, by whose choice he is living where he is, and what purpose there is for him in his being in care, may help point towards either rehabilitation to his own family, or placement in a new permanent family.

Where the child is with a foster home, then this role definition can be particularly painful as the foster parents may not have expected to take a child on permanently, and yet find it difficult to say that it is right for him to leave them and go to a permanent family. It takes a lot of courage, but it is essential that foster families do not become semi-adoptive families unless that is their real choice, and the child's. Both parties may have entered into the original arrangement believing it to be of limited duration. For that contract the arrangement may have been 'good enough'. When it drifts into permanence without the contract being redrawn, then there is a very real danger of the home 'disrupting' or breaking down in the stresses of adolescence.

So let's look at the prognosis for rehabilitation. If:

(a) the mother is emotionally mature;

(b) the child is loved and valued;

(c) the emotional climate of the home is good;

(d) reception into care was mainly to relieve personal or functional difficulties for the parents

and the relationship with the social worker is good, then work towards the child going home is likely to be successful. Each stress factor in the family, for example poor housing, mental and physical ill health, or financial inability, multiplies the problems, and likelihood of emotional disturbance in the child (Rutter 1975), and diminishes the possibility of successful rehabilitation.

Parents will need a contract of visiting that makes clear their involvement in and responsibility for their child and yet which does not create conflicts for the child in the 'in care' situation. Every breakdown of that contract needs your sympathetic evaluation. So often it is easy to gloss over a failure to visit with references to travel problems or time difficulties, without looking at the emotional blocks that are the root cause. The purpose and expectations of the visits should form part of the contract. Stress demonstrated by the child before and after parental contact should be recorded by carers. Similarly (and far less frequently done) a record should be kept of the positives and enjoyment of parental visiting. Conflicts for the parents in the reception they receive from carers should also be noted by them, or by the fieldworker, and efforts made for these to be resolved, possibly by discussion involving all the adults concerned.

The next major element to consider is the age of the child in care. If he is under 5 and has already had one major separation from his parents then the likelihood of successful rehabilitation is far smaller. This needs to be shared with the parents and planning regarding parental contact and support will be particularly crucial.

For the 5–11 age group the time factor and conflicts may not be quite so acute, but if 'shared care' is likely to continue beyond six months then your parental contract should detail expectations of the parent, child and carers. Help each of them to say what they would like of the others. Spend time with the parents, particularly just before a review, working out with them:

(a) why their child needs to remain in care;

(b) what anxieties they have about having him home;

(c) how soon they think the child should return home to live;

(d) how often they will see him in the next six months;

(e) how often and for how long they will have him home in the next six months;

(f) what they see as the purpose of (d) and (e);

(g) if he is not fostered, what the problems of offering him a family might be.

Adolescents may need considerable help to retain family links, particularly where they have been committed to care as being beyond the control of their parents. Although joint sessions of parent and child can be emotionally painful, a great deal of progress can be made in this way. The key residential worker may be an important part of these joint sessions, but where he is involved make sure that you and he have shared supervision before your next family contact. The adolescent's capability for manipulative splitting should never be underestimated! You and your colleague, working together with the family, need to be clear about your respective roles, and to share goals in treatment, if the difficulties are not to be exacerbated by your shared involvement.

The other aspect of family work with adolescents that I would recommend is to seek out the extended family. For many adolescents in care contact with cousins, aunts, uncles and grand-parents may provide a positive family identity they are unable to achieve through contact with their own parents. You will need, of course, to be aware of the wider family dynamics and conflicts. Help the youngster to invest some time with these other relatives and explain the long-term purpose of this to him. Remember the child abuse and suicide literature about the importance of lifelines of communication, and help the youngster to look beyond his 'in care' situation. Most adolescents tend to have their emotional focus in blinkers; yesterday, today and tomorrow are important, but longer term views are too overwhelming to be considered against the conflicts of the immediate. Peer relationships are crucial, adults less important. You may have to settle for giving written and pictorial information, but if possible try to take the youngster on visits as part of facilitating that contact for the future. Focus the interaction during such visits on the familial ties and activities of the family concerned.

The six-month issue

During the first six months that a child is in voluntary care his parents may remove him from care at any reasonable time and the authority does not have the right to retain the child in care against the parents' wishes, without seeking a change in the legal position through either taking parental rights and duties (Child Care Act 1980, Section 3) or wardship proceedings (Family Law Reform Act

1969). After he has been in care for six months his parents are required to give twenty-eight days' notice of their intention to remove the child from care, unless the local authority waives that requirement (Child Care Act 1980, Section 13 (2b)). If the local authority feels, that it is not in the interest of the child to return home, the twenty-eight days' notice gives the opportunity for legal action to be taken. There have been some test cases about the purpose of this period of notice, but the original idea has now been established in case law.

Parents must be told of the potential loss of their rights. Many local authorities have leaflets explaining this in some detail and there is an excellent model leaflet for parents in Leeding's *Child care manual for social workers* (1980) 4th edn, pp. 275–8. This part of the legislation can be used constructively with parents, as a focus to help all concerned decide future plans. The child also has the right to know of the potential change in the legal position; share it with him. Again, some authorities have produced leaflets that are given to each child in care and which give details of the various legal situations (Durham and Camden are good examples of this).

Reviews

The other six months' issue is that of reviews. Every child in care has to have a review at least every six months (Children and Young Persons Act 1969, Section 27) and if he is the subject of a care order the local authority is 'required to consider specifically whether or not it should apply for the order to be discharged by the court' (Leeding 1980). A review can be an information-sharing conference, pooling ideas and knowledge about a child, a planning session, or a time for shared decision-making. Every review should involve the child for at least part of the time, either personally or by means of a spokesman, preferably chosen by the child. As I write I am aware of the times that I have found reasons (or were they excuses?) for the child to be excluded. In practice there is a reluctance to call case conferences separately from reviews, because of the shortage of time of all concerned.

The issue of who should participate has also been raised by children in care (Page and Clark 1977). Alfred Leeding (1980) has expressed the hope that when the Secretary of State introduces regulations governing reviews (under Section 20 of the Child Care Act 1980) 'they will give clear guidance on the extent to which children and their natural parents should be involved as a matter of right'. Parents' presence may limit the scope of a review to a decision-making session, rather than one that includes information-sharing between professionals, but I would advocate their right to participate, particularly while the child remains in voluntary care.

The role of foster parents also raises some controversy. The National Foster Care Association point out that if foster parents are to be trusted with other people's children then we must also trust them with confidential information about both those children and their parents. They certainly need to be involved in all decision-making.

With regard to the involvement of teachers in reviews, the children of the 'Who Cares' group (Page and Clark 1977) point out that details of parental life and background are not generally available to teachers. Many children in care have felt themselves inappropriately handled by teachers who misunderstood their 'in care' situation. It is better for either the 'special' or fieldworker to form links with the school, akin to the role of the good natural parent. Educational difficulties can be recorded and reports sought for reviews where there have been particular problems.

Ideally a review should be chaired by someone who has no day-to-day management responsibility for the case. In practice the chairperson may be the senior supervising the fieldworker, or a residential adviser supervising the head of home. Where possible have present one person with no previous knowledge of the case, whose assignment is to challenge all habitual assumptions in the handling of the child.

A review is the time to examine the medical care a child is receiving. The parental medical history may give clues about specific health checks that should be carried out. Check that all illnesses, accidents and medical treatment have been recorded, not just on file but on something that will become the child's, as of right, when he leaves care. Details should include dates, doctors' names and addresses, hospitals, treatment given, prophylaxes received, etc.

Rights and duties

Section 3 of the Child Care Act 1980 grants to the local authority the right, in certain circumstances, to vest parental rights and duties in themselves by council decision, without a court hearing unless the parent appeals. It is the handling of this decision rather than its legal technicalities to which I wish to refer briefly. The council can be asked to take rights and duties from the day the child is received into care, but unless it is an emergency situation a review would be the proper place to decide that the council should be requested to take this action.

Where possible parents should be included in the decision-making process. The vesting of rights and duties in the council does not necessarily cut off all parental contact, but it removes the right to choose about their involvement from the parent and places it with the council. In some instances the parents are relieved to have the legal responsibility for their child lifted from them, but they may need help regarding the remaining financial liability. In all cases you should aim to discuss the whole matter with them thoroughly.

The legal phraseology of the documents informing parents that their rights have been assumed by the council can be very hurtful to parents. It is possible for you to deliver these personally, provided the parent still gives a written acknowledgement of receipt. If you have a continuing relationship with the parent, or if you seek this for the child for whom you are responsible, then take the documents yourself. Talk through the purpose of the action. You may have done this several times before the council's day of resolution, but this is still the day of bereavement for the parents. They may respond in unexpected or even inappropriate ways, but remember your knowledge of bereavement theory and help them to hold on to the positives of the action.

In some areas, rights and duties are taken on all children in care for three years. Remember the concept of a caring partnership. It may be important not to opt for legal security for the child and choose trust and reciprocity with parents as an alternative tool. At the other extreme, you need to ensure that your authority has a system for taking rights and duties on an emergency basis.

The child's wishes and feelings are to be considered in this, as in other aspects of care (Child Care Act 1980, Section 18), and he should be informed of the legislative change that the three-year period offers. A child may not want the council to take rights and duties. This is not binding, but it could appropriately delay your application while you work with the child to help him understand that your role with his parents *need* not cease as a result of making his own position more secure. Ideally the child's view should be expressed to council.

Try to write out for the child not only the legal grounds on which it is proposed, but also the thinking that lies behind it. While it may not be appropriate to give this to a young child at the time, it should be made available to him either when he is older, or when he is discharged from care.

Further reading
Adcock, M. and White, R. 1977, *The assumption of parental rights and duties*, Association of British Adoption and Fostering Agencies.

Visiting children in foster homes
While there are no specific regulations about children in establishments being visited by fieldworkers, the Boarding Out of Children Regulations, 1955, still apply as those laid down by the Secretary of State (Child Care Act 1980, Section 22) in respect of children in care who are placed with foster parents. While some of the concepts embodied in those regulations are now regarded as dated, the overall standards that they demand remain appropriate. A recent DHSS report (*The study of the boarding out of children*, 1982) has shown that despite the fact that work with foster homes and children in care is usually being undertaken by qualified social workers, the children who were boarded out 'received less attention than other children in care, less attention than the minimum requirements of the statutory regulations, and less attention than the objective reality of their situation warranted'.

I do not intend covering the enormous issues involved in placing children in foster homes, for you should obtain advice from your own specialist section in seeking and approving foster homes, and there is a vast literature already covering the issues of placement. A good handbook on working with foster homes, with all the basic principles clearly outlined, is the HMSO publication *Foster care – guide to practice* (1976). However, within a generic case-load you are likely to have responsibility for supervising children in long-term foster placements. What follows aims to help you in that task.

Private foster homes
Children can be placed with foster parents, by their own parents, without coming into care. These foster parents are often called 'CP' after the child protection legislation that used to be the statutes involved; alternatively, they are known as private foster homes. The legislation registration and supervision of such foster homes is now consolidated in the Foster Children Act 1980. There are at present no regulations under Section 3 in existence, so visiting the foster homes is at the discretion of the local authority. As a

guideline, use the Boarding Out of Children Regulations, 1955, which are those applying to children in local authority foster homes (see section entitled 'contact with social workers' in check-list 8).

All the financial arrangements, the medical care and educational progress of the child remain the responsibility of the natural parent, although they would also form part of your discussion with the foster mother. Your role may need to include liaising between the parent and the foster parent and helping to resolve conflicts (see 'conflicts in fostering' on p. 68). The major differences between private foster homes and local authority foster homes shown in Holman's study *Trading in children* (1973), are well summarised by Prosser (1978). The main points that are relevant to your practice are as follows:

Placements were made on the basis of advertisements or casual contacts and were without preparation; 94 per cent of the placements were notified to the local authority after they had commenced. Some 60 per cent of the children were legitimate West Africans, most of them under 5, having been placed before they were a year old. The private foster home was more likely than a local authority one to be overcrowded, the private foster father less involved with the fostering, and the foster children more likely to be emotionally deprived, shown by some extreme form of aggression, anxiety, difficulty in making relationships or withdrawal. The children were more likely to need special education. The natural parents were likely to visit once a month, to be poorly housed and of low income, with few relatives or contacts. They used the foster parents because they had no alternative. What is clear is that there should be at least as much work done with private foster homes as with children in care in local authority foster homes.

The problems of working with private foster homes include:

1. Finding a role that is not that of an inspector, while retaining the authority vested in the local authority to control the standards of care.

2. Helping the child in the emotionally conflicting atmosphere without jeopardising the placement. Many children who are privately fostered have been in several foster homes.

3. The lack of statutory guidelines to give clarity to all concerned about why you are visiting.

Try to work out a contract with the foster parent and child that makes some sense to both. Ensure you check the foster parent has all the basic information needed about the parents. Much of Chapter 3 is also relevant to this area of work. Also, encourage your local authority to develop a policy statement about work with private foster homes.

Local authority foster homes

Foster parents offer help to the department, but there is a tendency to treat them as subordinates, not worthy of our trust. I would differentiate between two kinds of long-stay local authority foster homes:

1. The foster parents who were chosen by the local authority, following a selection procedure that was probably considerably more rigorous than the interviews for your job! The child was then selected and only placed with them after careful and well-planned introductions.

2. The child was related to/knew/met and got to like/stayed with on a casual basis, and built up contact with, a family who then invited that child to go and live with them. Only at that point was a social worker involved in deciding whether they would be suitable foster parents.

The first category should clearly be treated as colleagues, which they cannot be unless you share openly with them. They cannot, for example, help the natural parent, unless problems are shared with him. This extension of confidentiality needs to be made explicit. Ideally, this kind of foster parent could be given a job description related to her task with a particular child.

The second kind of foster parent may present you with more problems. She may never have wanted to have a shared role with the department, have little understanding of your role, and in many cases want to work on an 'exclusive' basis, excluding the local authority and the natural parents from involvement with the child. There is likely to be an element of 'rescuing' the child from the 'orphanage' about their emotional orientation. I would not preclude these foster parents from child-care provision, for they may offer permanent substitute homes with stability and love, but the legal position they leave you in is extremely difficult, while the child remains in care. You are required to supervise the child and retain legal responsibility for his health, welfare, education and progress. When custodianship, under the Children Act 1975, is implemented then these are the kinds of situations that one would expect, after three years, to be recommended for custodianship, having used the three years to clarify the main areas of difficulty for the child that lie ahead. In the meantime it can be difficult to resolve the conflicts that these placements produce. If the foster family are relatives I would urge that the child should not be in care; instead the relatives should receive help under Section 1 of the Child Care Act 1980, on a six-monthly review basis. This leaves the child out of care, not fostered, with the responsibility for him firmly with the family and not with the local authority

Conflicts in fostering

The main sources of these (Orlin 1977) are as follows:

(a) foster parents feeling superior to the natural parent;

(b) natural parent feeling resentful of the foster parent;

(c) natural parents' resentment makes them behave defensively towards the foster parents;

(d) foster parents resent the social worker 'telling them how';

(e) the social worker being alert to the non-altruistic motives of the foster parents, who believe all their motives are altruisitic;

(f) the foster parent, natural parent and social worker each believe that they know the child best, and what is best for the child;

(g) the foster child feels ambivalent towards all the adults involved.

If you are finding supervising a foster home difficult, it can be helpful to go through the list and work out which ones apply.

Resolution of conflicts is best achieved by each recognising the legitimacy of the other's interest, and seeking to find a solution by persuasion, minimising differences and enhancing each other's understanding. The danger is that you will feel tempted to throw the departmental book at the foster parents, using strategies of power, threat and coercion, in situations where you feel very strongly about the child's welfare. Try instead to break down the conflict into separate issues, so that it is no longer all or nothing, and avoid talking about precedents that may be being set. Think instead of treating each situation as individual and encourage the foster parents to do the same. Wherever possible, stress commonalities between foster and natural parents, including communities, church, interests, etc. that may be shared. Above all, avoid threats to self-esteeem or claiming superiority. Where the natural parent is presenting conflicts for the child, or problems in the foster home, you should expect to play a part in resolving these.

Support for foster parents

Praise is not condescending, but the recognition of a job well done. Foster parents have the right to expect us to praise them for the child's development, skills, understanding of his own background, and his socialising capabilities. They need support and understanding when they cope with conflicts with natural parents, and when either the foster child or his parent is ill.

Your visits should, of course, be considerate, but, ideally, sometimes without notice. Include the foster father not less than one in three visits – too often he is only involved when there is a crisis and this under-values his contribution to the care of the child. Finances should form part of the discussion with foster parents – an issue that is often dodged. Remember that foster parents are saving the department a colossal amount of money. The current average cost of a child in a foster home nationally is less than one-third of the cost of a child in an average children's home (National Foster Care Association 1981). Become familiar with all the additional payments your authority offers, and make these available to the foster family and encourage them to mention them to you if you fail to offer them.

Family discipline is different from the way discipline needs to be handled in establishments. Because the local authority policy is against corporal punishment, should foster parents who smack their own small children not do this to small foster children? I would support foster parents using the same discipline methods with their foster children as they do with their own. These should be thoroughly explored with them and their children before they are approved. When you accept responsibility for the child placed in a foster home, as part of familiarising yourself with the case you should expect to know about the forms of discipline that are prevalent in the family.

Recording is a requirement of the regulations; include details of the child's health, welfare, conduct and progress as well as any problems that the foster parent may be experiencing. Unfortunately the regulations do not require you to specify the things that the foster parent is delighting in, but don't forget to include those, as they will be important as tools for strengthening the placement.

Many of the difficulties that occur between foster parents and field social workers are to do with a lack of understanding about the responsibilities of each. Some authorities issue excellent booklets for their foster parents, telling them of their rights and of the authorities' expectations. I think the basics of these are best outlined in a chart form, so I have included them at the end of the chapter as check-list 8 – Responsibilities in fostering.

Visiting children in establishments

As a fieldworker responsible for children in care who are placed in an establishment (your own authority's or a voluntary or independent home), you should expect to know certain basic facts about that home. I have listed these in check-list 7 at the end of the chapter. I don't suggest that you treat the list as if you were an inspector, but as a way of jogging your memory about the aspects of care that you may have been missing, and helping you to define your role with the child and the home.

When you summarise your case notes, try to include comments about the establishment that will make it 'come alive' to a colleague in later years, if the information needs to be drawn on for the child. Often records have comments about particular staff members who have been contacted, but nothing about the home itself. Ideally a profile of the home should form part of the basic information accumulated for the child.

Students from residential homes tell me that children do not like, or know what to do with, their field social workers, yet Kahan in *Growing up in care* (1979) quotes several adults who had valued the relationship they had with their fieldworkers. Consistency, clarity about why you are visiting and what you can offer, trustworthiness and the ability to reinforce the child's self-esteem are the essentials for the relationship you should aim to build with the child. Make clear how often you will visit and stick to it. Cancelling a visit to deal with a crisis will only show the child he has to have a crisis to be sure of you!

Try to see the child both in and out of the home. Share activities where possible; visits to the zoo or skating rink offer the child the opportunity to ask difficult questions in a relaxed, almost casual way. So does sharing the washing-up! The difficult balance is between the professional, authority-holding, parental figure and the befriending, enabling carer. Your activities with the child should be complementary to his own parents' role, and to the residential staff's. The child will test every aspect of your relationship, both verbally and physically, as he will your residential colleagues. Allow him to tease and try you out, without assuming that every part of what he says is seriously meant. In important areas, try to have time to check back or visit again, before a decision has to be made. Remember that it is difficult to tell simply from his behaviour at the time whether a child is telling the truth. He may be influenced by events of the day, or a friend's new craze. You and your residential colleagues need to record over a time-span a child's comments and reaction, links of pleasure and pain, and to check whether the child's behaviour confirms what is said and what occurs.

If time is short, write to the child before you visit. In the letter, outline the issues that have to be decided and suggest that the child discuss them with others before you come. All very obvious, but so easy to forget.

Keywork with children in long-term care

The level of supervision is the crucial factor in deciding who does the work that I am going to outline. In working intimately with a child about his own background, in preparing him for sharing appropriately about himself with the outside world, great care needs to be taken that the worker does not project his own perceptions and experience on to the child. You need to be aware of your own pain and losses experienced in childhood and to allow yourself to remember the despair and the partings. Which areas from your own life would be hard to share with a colleague? How would you help a child share a similar difficult loss? Does your colleague agree that this is not projecting your own responses? Try doing this kind of exercise in pairs in a group and discuss your findings with each other. It builds group trust appropriately, as well as increasing the sensitivity of your work with the children.

Any child in long-term care requires help in three basic areas of identity and knowledge. He needs to know (I don't mean superficially able to recite!) and accept the reason he is in care, to grasp all the details of that reason increasingly as he gets older. At 6 the knowledge can be given in simple terms, but at 13 he needs to be able to discuss it and explain it to a peer. He is likely to be very resistant to attempts to encourage discussion in this area. It is painful and can be embarrassing. Try doing a role play where you are him and he is his nosey friend asking all the questions. Get him to tell you when you say things he couldn't say himself. Try a scene at the disco, where his girl-friend asks him why he lives in the children's home, or why he never mentions his parents. Ask him where it is hardest for him to have people know (school, club, down the street) and help him plan ways of coping with the questions.

Those youngsters who seem to 'tell' happily may weave in a wide variety of lies, until the truth gets lost to themselves. Truth requires reinforcing, but not enforcing; it is not for us to 'blow' a child's cover, but to help him not to need to use it. Strengths in a family background need seeking and stressing. 'Just like your dad' is so often used as a pejorative that we forget how important it can be to underline what parents are good at, and to look for the 'just like' in these positive areas.

The second aspect is that of memories. These too need reinforcement. From his first six months' review, every child in care should have a photograph album. For a child placed in a foster home the album may underline a difference from the natural children. Urge the foster parents to give each of their own children their own album, or, if you can get agreement, supply them. It is regrettable, appalling and a statistic that incorporates a great deal of heartache and sorrow, but nearly 50 per cent of fostering placements break down. The child will need those photographs, labelled and dated, to hold on to the positives of the fostering experience if he has to leave. They are also a way of sharing his past with each new fieldworker!

Where you are able to do history building from the beginning of a child's period in care, the third area of knowledge the child needs will be mainly catered for. Many children in care do not have basic facts about their famiies. Carers and child alike in some cases have been ignorant of the names of his parents or grandparents, or whether he had any cousins.

Drawing a family tree with a child and family together needs care, for in that situation the child is free to ask about relatives whom he may previously never have heard of. As long as you are sure of your own capacity to hold the pain of what may be revealed, and are prepared to be quickly available to both child and family after such a session, this technique is a useful and revealing one.

The tree itself should not be a 'once done, put away for ever' document. Bring it out occasionally as part of your memory sharing. Try to obtain up-to-date information about those relatives mentioned, perhaps using a review as a reminder time. Has the possibility of their being more involved been explored recently? Is the reason they were unable to help still valid? In one case a new worker was told that an aunt and uncle of a child in care could not help because the aunt's aged mother needed full-time care. The worker discovered that the mother had died two years before and the aunt was in fact able, when encouraged and supported, to offer quite a lot of shared care, and therefore family identity, to the child.

As well as the photograph album, memory file and family tree, a child in care should have a life story book, that gives simple facts of his movements in care and includes addresses and dates for him. For those who have not had the photograph album or memory file kept during their early period in care, writing a life story book can be a helpful way of helping them to sort out their own history. The ABAFA book *Planning for children in long term care* (1976) gives a good example of this in 'The story of Steven Shore', while Dennis Eikenberry (1969) describes the impact writing 'A story for Mary' had on a child in foster care. He ends: 'Writing a book about a child's life experiences makes them graphic and tangible for the child and the worker. The book can be used to present therapeutic material of a sophisticated nature on a level that is meaningful and real to a very young child.'

A simple rendering of the same idea can be accomplished by a flow chart, and where good photographic records and memory files have been kept this may be preferred as a simple tool to work with.

When you take over responsibility for a child from another worker it can sometimes be difficult to get to know him. Try doing a poster about himself with him (Figure 5.1). Fill in the easy parts first, like 'favourite colours' and 'things I like'. Remember that lots of different colours will add to the visual impact and that the object is not to practise writing skills! If these are limited, offer to do the writing for him and suggest cutting out pictures from magazines and catalogues to illustrate his poster. This technique can also be helpful in preparing a child for moving from an establishment to a new placement, as it gives a focus for new staff or carers to discuss with the child.

'Chronic' child care cases

These are characterised by several volumes of files and a large number of social workers having been responsible for them over the years. They often consist of several children, not always placed together, not necessarily all in care. I have devised a check-list to help you look at why the case has become chronic and what you might do about it, to try and get a new focus to the work you undertake (see check-list 5).

Adolescents in care

As well as the three basic areas of knowldge mentioned before, an

Poster about David

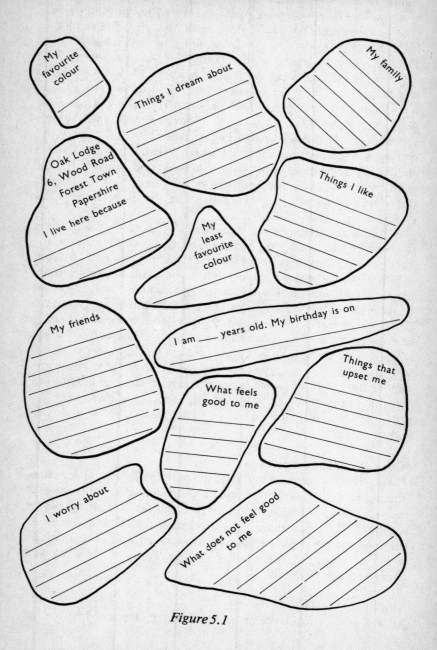

Figure 5.1

adolescent in care needs other kinds of 'know how'. Your first task would be to define who should be the appropriate worker for each of the following areas:

Boundary setting: Who set the boundaries in childhood, for this adolescent? Is that person still around? Can the adolescent use them to rebel against? Has that person moved on? If so, who can take on the role? Were the boundaries set appropriate? Only at home? In the current placement?

Peer relationships. Who are they with? Where does delinquency/conformity come? Do the norms need influencing? Is the adolescent's sexual identity clarifying? Do his sexual relationships need any help? Does he have contacts in the community? Would youth clubs, evening classes or activities help?

Health: Does he know how to register with a GP? About hospitals and how they work? About sexual responsibility? Venereal disease and the 'special clinics'? Contraception? Who is helping him understand about self-care in terms of diet, hygiene, etc.?

Education/employment: Clarify the aspirations of the child, the parent, the residential social worker or foster parent. Whose model does the child wish to emulate? Whose responsibility will this be?

Accommodation: Establish which neighbourhood is the important one to the child. Link choice of living area with employment and education aims. Discuss tenancy responsibilities. Look at areas of responsibility for cleaning and keeping his own room tidy, responsibility regarding noise and nuisance.

Money: Does the child understand about saving? How to save? Where to save? Post Office and building society and bank methods? A week in hand? Being paid monthly? Who is helping him practise budgeting? Costing food for one? Living on benefit? Does he know how and where to claim supplementary benefit? Where to 'sign on'? Does he have practice in managing independence and know what 'lifeline' resources are available from the council?

When you are working with an adolescent who has just come into care, remember that however bad the home circumstances may be, the child has part of the family in himself and will need help to work out which are the bits he wants to hold on to and which parts he wants to change, or throw away. In a few years he will need his own family, he will be out of care, and will need to resolve the conflicts about how much contact he wants long term. Try to define with the adolescent and the parent which parental roles they will retain and which of the areas above they will work with. Think how the parent and child links can be, or should be, reinforced. There is a real danger of collusion with the adolescent against the parent, particularly where one's own adolescence is still unresolved. Be aware of this danger and check it constantly with your supervisor.

In forming contracts with adolescents recognise the transience of their problems and the disproportionate importance they assume *today*. Try not to collude with this while bearing in mind that a caring parent allows for mistakes and the capacity to learn from them. Local authorities are not good at allowing children to make mistakes while in their care, particularly in the area of personal expenditure!

Finally, remember that the fieldwork task with children in care should be varied and tailored to each child's individual needs, dependent on his circumstances. Ensure that you and the child know what purpose your role is serving. It is often a separateness, in which to discuss his familial situation, which he prefers to leave out of the day-to-day living situation. It should include a plan for his long-term future, looking forward to the day when he will be integrated in a community, with long-term friends and connections to support his adult life. Your job is to facilitate this integration, not to remove the responsibility for its accomplishment from the youngster concerned.

Check-list 6 – *Chronic cases*

Diagnosis – the reason it is chronic

Family

1. How far does intractable poverty: (a) give a permanent reason for the need for help; (b) mean that the problem is not reachable?

2. *Why* is money mismanaged? Is there enough emotional strength to reverse patterns? What alternative satisfactions could be offered?

3. What part does housing actually play? Provide an excuse for . . . ?

4. How large a part is played by physical distance between family and child in preventing rehabilitation? What help have they had in overcoming this?

5. Is the family fulfilling a role into which they have been cast?

Child

1. In an establishment because . . . ??? How much is this a reflection of: (a) Prejudice against fostering? Whose? (b) Lack of imagination? (c) Lack of energy?

2. Can't go home because . . . ??? When was that last tested? If recently, then how has the focus with the home changed since then? What is the current purpose of work with home? Is there a clear contract, defining roles in the shared care arrangements?

3. Has the child the capacity to change? To relate? To choose? Has the child been asked what he wants from the social worker? Told what the social worker can offer?

4. How does the child view home? Siblings? Is placement with the siblings vital?

What can I do?

Identify what part of the burden of the case bothers you most by:

(a) examining which areas you work on most frequently/most willingly/least;

(b) looking at all members of the family and working out a pattern of relationships, including relationships with the social worker and with the agency;

(c) looking at your use of time – what are you doing instead of: (i) Delegating? (ii) Planning? (iii) Thinking?

Select:
(a) A goal your client (the child) or his parents can share and use a contract to achieve it;

(b) An objective to work on with the child in care – e.g. why does he hate school? Why does he not persist in any leisure activity outside the children's home?

(c) One area of relationship to work with, e.g. (i) the cause of problems in John's relationship with his residential social worker; (ii) mother's compulsive need to have babies, that stops John coming home;

(d) A new client focus, e.g. work with father instead of mother, with grandparents instead of either.

Seek to share a case with:
(a) a colleague giving a defined area of work to each of you and meeting

regularly to discuss. This contributes additional professional skills as well as offering you stimulus;

(b) a volunteer to do a particular part of the case;

(c) a voluntary organisation who may be able to undertake some specialised work with either the child, e.g. Barnardo's 15 + project, working with adolescents towards independence; or with the parents, e.g. Family Service Unit, working on family relationships in a more intensive way than your case-load allows. If the family has moved a long way away it may be more appropriate to involve a local agency to work with them, with whom you can liaise.

Recording

Summarise the volumes – decide to give one month's interviewing time to doing this *instead* of interviewing, explaining this to all concerned. From the patterns discovered, form a list of headings under which to record in future, using them to define areas of work and progress.

Reviews

Use them to focus: (a) who does what; (b) why the establishment view of the child is different from yours/the parents'.

Define a keyworker for each client within the family, rather than you trying to be all things to everyone.

Check how many changes of social workers and 'two-year attempts' have failed, and consider again whether it is now appropriate to change: (a) focus; (b) placement; (c) who has the right to choose; (d) whose choice has precedence.

Check-list 7 – *Establishments*

What you should aim to know

(You never will know it all but it helps to check on what you are missing out.)

Organisation

Who to communicate with about (a) placement; (b) visiting; (c) reviews; (d) changes in parental situation.

How many children are catered for in the establishment, age range, sex ratio, ethnic range and balance.

Children/staff ratio on duty at different times of the day, particularly bedtime, early morning, and coming in from school times.

Who sleeps in? How are sleeping-in duties organised? How does this affect relationships and delegation?

Calibre of staff?

Is there a system of 'specialising'?

Cultural

What is the local areas's predominant social class and ethnic grouping? Do the children in the establishment differ proportionately?
What is the area's response to the children?
What club and local resources are available? Encouraged? Frowned on?

Communal

How much does the individual child have to share, e.g. playclothes? Toys?
How are privacy, quiet, noise, action allowed, and where?
Who chooses TV programmes, clothes, activities, food, decorations in the house?
Are there any children's meetings? Staff meetings? When? Can you go too?

Bedroom facilities

How many to a room? Quality and quantity of bedding? Who chooses? Use of colour?
Privacy and sharing – how is naturalness balanced?
How and where are belongings kept? Who does the mending, ironing, etc.?
Does each child know who to go to in a crisis in the night?
Wash/W.C. facilities – how near are these to the bedroom, and how appropriate is any segregation?

Education

Where? Who liaises with school or education authority? What kinds of school are available? Are there any problems with the local education department?

Health

Medical advice, examination and specialism available? Medical record for the child kept as well as for the establishment?

Food

Mealtime patterns – how important is it, or easy, for the child to go out? To have the social worker in? To have friends in? Who can make meals? Tea, coffee, squash? When? Where?

Religion

Does the establishment have a particular faith? How many staff are practising members of it? Where and in what degree is this practised? What outside help is available for what faiths?

Fire

Staff awareness of hazards? Last fire drill held when? Records held in a fireproof cabinet?

Relationships

Who chooses 'specials' (keyworkers) if they exist? Who does the child relate most closely to? Who creates the most negatives in the child? How important are peers in the establishment? What do staff call social worker? What does child call social worker?

The following areas may be helpful to consider staff attitudes towards: (a) Bathtime – who says when, how long, how often? (b) Bedtime – set? Flexible? Punishment? (c) Bedwetting – who strips the bed? Washes the sheets? Where? (d) Cleanliness – how vital and why? (e) Dirt – how allowable? (f) Getting up – whose responsibility? What time? (g) Illness – who cares? How acceptable/allowable is it to be ill? Meals in bed? (h) Locking up – by whom? At what time? What happens if the child is late in? (i) Lying in – allowed? How often? Until when? (j) Mealtimes – how vital? What sanctions? What freedom? (k) Scruffiness – OK? When? (l) Sex – feared/accepted in the children? Hetero only? (m) Smoking – OK? When? (n) Telephone – who may use which? For what? For how long? (o) Temper – how much? By whom? Against whom? (p) Touch – OK by whom? How much? Who says so? (q) Unemployment – OK? How long? What pressure? What help?

Do staff believe in: (a) Allowing children choice? (b) Playing with children? (c) Parental importance? (d) Parental acceptance? (e) Parental sharing? (f) Corporal punishment? (g) Other punishment – what kind? (h) Rewards? (i) Sharing selves with the children? (j) Talking and listening to children?

Check-list 8 Responsibilities in fostering

Subjects: Allowances, including clothing and holidays; birthdays, Christmas, consents, contact with parents, contact with social workers, dental treatment, earnings (see wages), education, emergencies, food, medicals, moving house, past history, police, religion, removal of a child, reviews, wages.

SUBJECT	1. THE FOSTER PARENT'S RESPONSIBILITIES	2. THE LOCAL AUTHORITY OR FIELD SOCIAL WORKER'S RESPONSIBILITIES
Allowances *Fortnightly payment* Payments to foster parents are often made as part of fortnightly computer 'run'. Payment is for a week in advance and a week in arrears. This is not immutable, despite administrative pressures to convince you that it is! Each authority determines its own rate of pay to foster parents despite pressure from National Foster Care Association for a national rate, with urban 'weightings'.	To let you know if the fortnightly payment is presenting them with any problems. To let you know before the foster child spends time away from the foster home (see Consents). A retainer may be payable, but in some authorities it is the foster parent's responsibility to negotiate this. To let you know when the child starts earning as the allowance may need to be adjusted (see Wages). To give the foster child weekly pocket-money, encouraging him to use it responsibly.	To make sure the foster parent's payment arrives, and that s/he knows what is included in the basic rate. To notify the foster parent of any change in the rates because of birthdays or increased allowances. To arrange an alternative method of payment if the fortnightly one is inconvenient for the foster parent. To give a guideline as to what amount of pocket-money is appropriate, and discuss with the foster parent how this fits in with her own family arrangement about pocket-money.

SUBJECT	1. THE FOSTER PARENT'S RESPONSIBILITIES	2. THE LOCAL AUTHORITY OR FIELD SOCIAL WORKER'S RESPONSIBILITIES
Each authority has its own system of extras to the basic allowance.	To keep the child clothed like their own, normally from the basic, inclusive boarding out rate. To let you know if clothing is a problem due to sudden growth, behaviour difficulties, special needs or interests, including uniforms, athletics kit, etc. To help the child gain independence in choosing clothes on a budget; to share with him the fact of the clothing allowance and help him clothe himself within it.	When necessary, to make an initial clothing allowance available. To keep clothing allowance realistic in view of economic pressures and rising prices, and keep foster parent informed of the amount of the basic allowance which is regarded as being for clothing. To offer extra allowances for change of school necessitating uniform purchase, other uniforms, sports equipment and for big items for adolescents, e.g. winter coats. To let foster parent know what possible 'extras' to the basic allowance are available. These can include special payments for particularly difficult children; paying for a telephone to be installed and paying for the rental, either where a child needs particularly to remain in contact with a parent by phone, or where the foster parent will take emergency cases; paying for laundry costs for an enuretic child, etc.

Most authorities have additional allowances for holidays.

To tell you the dates, addresses and cost of the holidays that are planned, and the cost of travel. If foster parents are planning to go abroad they should be asked to give as much notice as possible because of the delays that can be occasioned in obtaining the relevant consents and passport for their foster child.

To tell the foster parent of the allowances available and where necessary to negotiate special allowances for special circumstances. To know where, when and how the foster parent is taking the child for whom you are responsible. To send the cheque for the holiday allowance in good time. To obtain appropriate consents: (i) for a child in care Section 2 – from parents; (ii) for a child in care Section 3 – from a senior member of the department or possibly committee; (iii) for a child who is the subject of a care order – if going abroad the courts' consent may be needed; check your local policy on how long a holiday abroad a child may have without a court consent.

Birthdays

To help the child to celebrate in a way that is like their own children's birthdays, bearing in mind that this can embarrass the child or his parents. To give him a present and a card, and discuss with the child differences between what his own family can or do provide and what he receives in the foster family.

To consult with foster parent about gifts from the social worker to the child and consider whether this is appropriate.

SUBJECT	1. THE FOSTER PARENT'S RESPONSIBILITIES	2. THE LOCAL AUTHORITY OR FIELD SOCIAL WORKER'S RESPONSIBILITIES
Christmas Local authorities vary as to whether they give a special allowance for Christmas and if so how much.	To use the allowance received for the extras for the child for Christmas. To discuss with you any particular need the child may have for a more expensive present. To discuss with you whether you should give the child a present in addition to those received within the foster home (dependent on your relationship with the child). To be sensitive to any conflict in the child about whether to spend Christmas in the foster home or with own parents, and also any conflicts between style of foster parent Christmas and own home Christmas.	To make sure Christmas allowance arrives early in December. To discuss with foster parent whether a present from the social worker is appropriate. To help the foster parent resolve any conflicts between parental Christmas and foster home.
Consents	To obtain from the social worker when appropriate consent of the natural parent or the Director of Social Services for any of the following unless the department has given a written agreement that the foster parent may give such consent: immunisation;	To ensure that the foster parent understands how long such consents may take to obtain. To make available an emergency service and let the foster parent know how to obtain consents when the social worker is not available.

Policy about children going to stay overnight with friends from foster homes varies. Some authorities delegate the right to make this decision to the foster parents, some require the consent of the local authority for any stay, anywhere other than in the foster home.

anaesthetics and operations; obtaining passports; going abroad; apprenticeships; going into the forces. To notify the local authority of *any* nights the child will be staying away from the foster home, and with whom.

Where necessary or appropriate to seek references on people with whom the foster child may go to stay. The balance between the child's welfare and the need for the child to lead a life that is as normal as possible on the one hand and the public accountability for the child's whereabouts and safety is a difficult one. Above all, policy must be clear to the foster parents and some contractual arrangement reached. Try to do this before the issue is raised regarding a particular incident. Be ready to discuss the problems with the foster child.

Contact with parents

To make parents feel welcome to their home and to make the visits as comfortable as possible for parent and child. Where possible to make occasion for the child and parent to have somewhere they can be private together. To help the child over his distress when his parents leave and not fall into the temptation of thinking it would be easier if parents didn't come at all. To discover and stress to the child the 'strengths' of his natural parents.

To help parents be considerate in their contact with foster parents. Where necessary to regulate parental visits as appropriate to the child's needs. To sort out muddles and conflicts between foster parent and natural parent. To provide travel warrants, and/or cash for fares for parents to visit. In exceptional circumstances to arrange for the parents and children to meet somewhere other than at the foster home. To help foster parents understand the natural parents and find their 'good points'.

SUBJECT	1. THE FOSTER PARENT'S RESPONSIBILITIES	2. THE LOCAL AUTHORITY OR FIELD SOCIAL WORKER'S RESPONSIBILITIES
Contact with social workers	To ask the social worker to visit if she is concerned about any difficulty with the child. To make it possible for the social worker and child to talk on their own, or go out together. To discuss with the social worker the purpose and focus of her visits, and not turn them into polite entertaining sessions.	To be trustworthy, when foster parents share the difficulties they are experiencing. To comply with regulations about visiting:
	To share with the social worker the delights and frustrations of caring for the child. To feel sufficiently secure with the social worker to share the problems without fear of being blamed, or that the child will be summarily removed.	*Short stay* (i.e. child in foster home for less than eight weeks). Visit within two weeks of arrival and not less than every four weeks. Visit immediately if any complaint is received about or from the child.
		Long stay (i.e. child is staying longer than eight weeks). Visit before a child is placed in the home, within a month of placement and then:
		Children under 5 – every six weeks for first two years and three-monthly thereafter; children over 5 and under school leaving age – every eight weeks for the first two years and three-monthly thereafter; children over school leaving age – not necessarily visit the foster home, but see the child within three months of leaving school and every three months thereafter.
		Visit within a month of a change of address and immediately if there is a complaint about or from the child. These are the minimum and usually you

Dental treatment

To ensure that at least six-monthly checks are carried out through school or family dentist and let the social worker know where these are being done.

In exceptional circumstances to pay for any additional costs involved.

Earnings (see Wages)

Education

It is the responsibility of the local authority where the child is living to provide appropriate education for the child's needs. If the child is placed with foster parents outside your own authority's boundaries then it is the responsibility of the local authority in which the foster parents live to provide for that child's needs, including special education.

Short stay: If possible the child should attend his own school. If not, foster parent and social worker agree on a local school and policy about school attendance.

Long stay: This would normally be part of the shared planning with the social worker. Foster parent needs to feel confident about recommending local schools. To attend parent/teacher meetings and liaise with school about difficulties. To tell social worker of all this and understand that social worker needs to be in touch with the school as well.

To liaise with and inform the local education department of the foster child's whereabouts. To assist foster parent in getting child into school, preferably of foster parents' choice. To liaise with the school that the foster child attends, or arrange with the foster parent how this liaison will be undertaken.

To arrange any specialist services, like child guidance clinic or psychological investigation.

SUBJECT	1. THE FOSTER PARENT'S RESPONSIBILITIES	2. THE LOCAL AUTHORITY OR FIELD SOCIAL WORKER'S RESPONSIBILITIES
Emergencies Each authority will have its own emergency procedure. These are to give you the basic areas to check.	To contact the department immediately if in need of assistance or advice. If the foster child is missing, or has an accident or has to go to hospital, or there is a crisis with the natural parents, they should contact an emergency number.	To ensure that foster parents have details of whom to contact in an emergency. To respond as quickly and as clearly as possible to any calls for help. To decide (unless this decision has been specifically delegated to the foster parents) whether/when a child who is missing from a foster home should be notified to the police.
Food	To know and understand that this may be a sensitive area for a child, who may experience a considerable change in diet from his own home or children's home, in coming to share the foster parents'. To share any difficulties experienced with the social worker.	To let the foster parent know of any dietary rules which the child may need to observe, e.g. vegetarian, Kosher, no beef, etc. and discuss with the foster parent any implications this may have for family life. To make available to foster parents details of different cultures' own eating and recipes and encourage those fostering children of a racial group other than their own to explore the food of that culture.

Medicals

| The regulations specify that a child's health forms part of the consideration of his welfare and suggest that reports on his health be interpreted by the community physician or a medical adviser. | To tell the social worker of *all* medical treatment that the child receives and help to maintain a personal medical record for the child. To take the child for an annual medical at the request of the authority. | To keep on file details of all milestones and illnesses and accidents. To supply the foster parent with the form for an annual medical and pay the GP's fee for this. To facilitate any specialist treatment that the child may need and obtain reports on this. |

Moving house

| Some authorities will help foster parents with removal to a larger house, both financially or in providing a larger house for rent. | To tell the social worker the new address as far ahead of the move as possible. | To visit foster parent and child within a month of the move and see around the new home. Where appropriate to notify the natural parent of the child's new address. To help with any new needs for the foster child that the move may have occasioned. |

Past history

| | To let a child's own past be a natural part of his thinking, not inhibiting him in talking about his own home, culture, parents, family, doubts and fears. To know enough about the child's background to be able to enjoy talking about these things in an intelligent way, which will let the foster child be relaxed about them too. | To give the foster parents enough written material to refer to about the child's background so that they may be able to answer the child's questions comfortably. To help with advice about culture and family relationships, offering discussion about difficult areas like a parent in prison or mental hospital and how such facts should be handled. |

SUBJECT	1. THE FOSTER PARENT'S RESPONSIBILITIES	2. THE LOCAL AUTHORITY OR FIELD SOCIAL WORKER'S RESPONSIBILITIES
Police	To let the social worker or the emergency duty officer know if the foster child is involved with the police. The police are not entitled to question or take a statement from a child without a responsible adult present.	To decide whether a social worker needs to be present at the police station as well as the foster parent. To make whatever arrangements are necessary for legal representation.
Religion	To come to an agreement with the social worker about what religious education and participation is appropriate for the child in her care.	The local authority is legally required to ensure that the child receives the religious upbringing he would have received while in the care of his parents or in accordance with his parents' wishes.
Removal of a child This is always an area of anxiety for foster parents, and they need written confirmation of what legislation applies and of what help they can call on if in difficulties.	To know when the child may go away from the foster home, and on whose say-so. To be clear about which relatives or friends are allowed to take a child out on a visit, etc. To prevent anyone, even a parent, from removing a child from her care, until she has the consent of the social worker emergency duty officer or other representative of	To discuss plans for the removal or discharge of a child from care in detail with foster parents and help them to plan this in a way that will be in the best interests of the child. To give clear dates and details about who may collect the child. Normally to accompany the person who is collecting the child, unless the foster parents are very sure that their

the social services department. If necessary the police will help this to be enforced, if a wait is necessary.

Reviews

To be aware that reviews are a statutory obligation on all children in care, three months after placement in a foster home and six-monthly thereafter. To participate with the social worker in planning the information recorded at these reviews. To assist in the planning for the child's welfare by sharing honestly the difficulties and the joys of the placement.

relationship with the person collecting the child is so good that the social worker's presence is superfluous. (*Note:* This should be the foster parents' decision, not the social worker's.) To offer information about the child to the foster parents after the child has left them, and to endeavour to establish continuing communication lines of an informal nature for this information to continue to reach the foster parent.

To invite foster parents to participate in reviews either on paper or by joining in a conference in the foster home or at the office. To ensure that at least once a year the foster home is visited by a reviewing officer who does not normally visit the foster home as a supervising officer. To send copies of the review forms to the foster parents for them to share with the foster child.

SUBJECT	1. THE FOSTER PARENT'S RESPONSIBILITIES	2. THE LOCAL AUTHORITY OR FIELD SOCIAL WORKER'S RESPONSIBILITIES
Wages Often a difficult area, as foster parents rightly wish to encourage the child to earn, without themselves losing the allowances they receive.	To let the social worker know when the foster child starts earning, as the amount paid as boarding-out allowances may have to be altered. To provide the name and address of the employer and details of earnings. To help the child learn to pay his way at home, budget and save, preparing him for adult responsibility.	To explain clearly what effect wages will have on boarding-out allowances. In many authorities Saturday earnings, or similar part-time wages, do not affect the over-all allowance, and only when the foster child enters full-time employment is the boarding-out allowance altered. When the foster child is in full-time employment a certain amount of his wage will be paid by him to the foster parent and the allowance paid by the authority reduced by that sum. Responsibility lies with the social worker to ensure that the sum payable by the child to the foster parent is actually paid. Differences between 'own children' contributions to foster home finances and foster children contributions need to be discussed fully and an equitable solution proposed, if necessary seeking special consent from senior members of the department. Tools, equipment and uniforms or special clothing for work should all form part of the over-all financial agreement reached with child and foster parent when the youngster starts work.

Exercise – Reviews

Robert (aged 15) and Diana (aged 12) Hill are both living in a small 'family' community home, The Briars, run by a residential social worker, Miss Vale (aged 55), who acts more as a foster parent, never taking her holidays, and sharing her life with all the seven children in the home. There is an assistant, Christine Street (aged 22), a peripatetic residential social worker, Michael Lane (aged 28), and a domestic, Mrs Rhodes (aged 48). Mrs Rhodes has worked at The Briars for ten years and helps in the child care. Christine and Michael have been employed there six months and eighteen months respectively. The Briars are going to Majorca for their holiday this summer.

Robert is the subject of a care order, following abuse by his mother. He has lived at The Briars since he was 4. Diana was received into care by another authority, who took rights and duties on the grounds of the mother's mode of life. Parental wherabouts have not been known for eight years, but the bond with Miss Vale and the various 'behaviour difficulties' which she stresses were felt to preclude fostering, whenever this has been suggested.

Robert is at a local secondary school and the year tutor sees him as very difficult. Miss Vale says he has no problems, and written school reports vary from teacher to teacher regarding Robert's behaviour and ability. Diana goes to middle school where she has remedial maths. She also attends child guidance clinic once a week as she bedwets about two nights in seven and often has bad nightmares. Miss Vale does not get on with the child guidance clinic social worker, Miss Torr.

Army Cadets is Robert's main social activity. He also has a 'social aunt and uncle', Mr and Mrs Bush, who have told you, but not Miss Vale, that Robert has been quite difficult lately. Diana has her own 'social aunt and uncle', Mr and Mrs Bull. Four weeks ago she refused to go to them any more. No reason has been given by Diana and the Bulls are upset.

You are the social worker for both youngsters, supervising Diana on behalf of the other authority. You liaise with a senior social worker, Miss Hampstead, regarding financial matters for Diana.

Task

Plan: (a) who should be there for the whole of the review on both children; (b) who should come for which part of each child's review; (c) who should invite whom and why.

What areas do you want to be sure are covered in the review? What work do you: (a) think you may need to do in the next two months; (b) anticipate needing to discuss at review?

6 Going Out of Care

> One point about providing an experience of acceptance and belonging for a youngster who has missed out on this is the immense problem of terminating the experience. Our feeling is that this experience is so vital to youngsters who have suffered repeated rejection that we have made it a cornerstone of our programme that they are free to attend as long as they like. (Alm 1981)

This comment from Intermediate Treatment is none the less true of youngsters leaving residential care and the feelings of fear, anxiety and loss are well expressed by those who participated in the 'Who Cares' group (Page and Clark 1977). This in this chapter I aim to look at some of the ways in which the trauma of leaving care can be lessened by the role and planning of the fieldworker.

The legislative framework for leaving care is as complex as that for entering it. I have once again reduced it to chart form (Table 6.1), showing the link between entry and discharge, but this is over-simplified and the legislative implications of discharge from long-term care would always need full discussion with someone well versed in the child-care legislative field.

Children who have come into care under Section 2 of the Child Care Act 1980 can, during their first six months in care, go home at any reasonable time at the request of their parents. The welfare of the child would govern the appropriateness of the time and suddenness with which this would be undertaken, but the social worker has no legal right to withhold information about the child's whereabouts, nor to prevent the parent removing the child, unless she obtains a place of safety order or take parental rights and duties. If a parent discharges a child from care in a way that the social worker considers unreasonable, or against social work advice, then this should be recorded. A number of such discharges may constitute a case for rights and duties to be taken. If he is being advised not to take his child from care, a parent should always be informed of the reasons for that advice, and this should be put in writing and given to the parent.

After the child has been in care six months, then under Section 13 (2)(b) of the Child Care Act 1980, either the parent must give twenty-eight days' notice or the local authority must consent to the child's discharge on an earlier date. As the social worker responsible, you will be aware of the implications of the

Table 6.1 Routes out of care

CHILD CARE ACT 1980
Section 2(3) In care less than six months – discharged to parent, guardian or relative at their request

Section 13(2) In care more than six months – discharged with local authority's consent or after 28 days' notice from parent

Discharge at age 18 – no further assistance wanted by child

Sections 27(1) and 29 At 21 years no longer eligible for financial help, except to complete a course already started. No longer eligible for befriending and assistance

Section 3 Resolution rescinded by local authority

CHILDREN AND YOUNG PERSONS ACT 1969
Order discharged by court on application by subject of the order or by the local authority

Care order made before 16th birthday – discharge at 18

Care order made after 16th birthday – discharge at 19

FAMILY LAW REFORM ACT 1969
Order varied by the court

MATRIMONIAL CAUSES ACT 1973
Order varied or discharged by the court

DOMESTIC PROCEEDINGS AND MAGISTRATES COURT ACT 1978
Order varied or discharged by the court

ADOPTION ACT 1958
Child adopted

CHILDREN ACT 1975
Section 33 (when implemented) Custodianship order made

GUARDIANSHIP ACT 1973
Order varied or discharged by the court

requirement that the welfare of the child should come first in considering whether to give consent for early discharge. The decision not to require the twenty-eight days may not be delegated to your senior. There is increasing pressure that consents of this nature should lie outside the direct management line, so that the interests of the child can be put first.

A written notice from the parent is advisable, although if literacy is a problem you can write it for them. In some authorities there is a *pro forma*. A telephone call can be regarded as notice, so be sure to record any such verbal request and discuss its implications with your senior.

If parental rights and duties have been taken, then the decision about the child going out of care before his eighteenth birthday will not be yours. He may be able to go 'home on trial' for weekends, short stays etc., with just your supervisor's consent, but the social services committee who took the resolution will have to pass another for the rights and duties to be rescinded. In some authorities the committee would want an interim report on the child's progress while home on trial, before considering a rescission.

Where a care order has been made on a child in the juvenile court, whether on criminal or care proceedings, then if the order was made before his sixteenth birthday, unless revoked before, it will last until the child is 18. If made on or after his sixteenth birthday it lasts until he is 19. Make sure you explain this to the youngster, as most of them quickly pick up the 18 'deadline' and make wrong assumptions about the duration of their own order. A care order can, of course, be revoked by a court at any time, although where the local authority and the parents are in agreement that the care order should be revoked, it is possible for the court to appoint a guardian *ad litem* to investigate the circumstances and ensure that it is in the best interests of the child that he should go out of care (Children and Young Persons Act 1969, Section 32). This is happening mainly where the child is too young to express his own views to the court. The guardian may be a social worker from another authority, a probation officer or an independent social worker.

A child who is the subject of a care order can go 'home on trial' on the decision of someone in your authority, and without recourse to the court. You will need to check at what level that decision-making power lies. A child should not even spend overnight at home without that person being consulted. If the child, who is subject to a care order, wants to go on holiday out of England and Wales then you may need to get the court's consent. Certainly, if the proposed holiday is for longer than three weeks you should consult the court and not just your internal decision-maker. I once got caught with a child returning to the West Indies, ostensibly for a holiday, and never returning. It is a fast way to a very red face in court!

While either the local authority or the child would apply in a juvenile court for the care order to be revoked, in the matrimonial courts it would normally be the parent who wishes to resume care or control who would apply for revocation. It could, however, be a grandparent or other relative who applies.

Wardship is quite different from all other court order situations, and although the order is still called a care order, it should be treated as a kind of shared care, where any decision to move a child, including returning him home, would need presentation to the court for ratification before the child was moved.

Borstal orders cause some confusion as to whether a child is in or out of care. If the Borstal order is made before his sixteenth birthday then it automatically cancels a care order. If, however, as is more general, the Borstal order is made after the sixteenth birthday, then the youngster remains in care and often the local authority will undertake after-care work. If you do not wish to do this, feeling that probation would be the more appropriate agency, then it will be necessary for the care order to be revoked. As a youngster who is discharged from care after his seventeenth birthday has certain additional rights to the one who is discharged at 16 (see check-list 9), it may be appropriate to delay revocation of the care order until after his seventeenth birthday.

Emigration does not necessarily constitute a discharge from care. Supervision can be undertaken by social service agencies in the country to which the child is going. A report on the home conditions and supervision available may be obtained through International Social Service of Great Britain, and the consent of either the committee or the court would have to be sought before the child left the country. Some children have moved abroad with their foster families. Children subject to care orders have gone 'home on trial' to their parents who are living abroad. Obviously the quality of supervision in the country of destination will determine whether the committee or court feel that it is advisable for the child to go, and whether the child needs to remain under English jurisdiction.

It is important to remember that, contrary to various myths, propagated by irresponsible authorities and bad social workers, help for those who have been in care does not have to end at 18. Perhaps that gauntlet needs challenging a little. Help in the sense I have used it there means the availability of befriending, advice, assistance financially with training and maintenance costs – in fact all the parental functions for the 16 + group, except love. Sadly for the 18 + it does not, legally, include holidays, unless you can get them counted as education or training! The ability to help financially is separate from the opportunity to advise and befriend at the youngster's request, although many authorities do attach some 'strings' to the financial help they offer.

Any child on being discharged from care at any age has the right, under Section 1 of the Child Care Act 1980, to advice, guidance and assistance from the local authority. These powers can be used imaginatively to bridge the gap between home and care, particularly where the child will be materially worse off with his parents than he would be if he remained in care.

The social work task

When a child is leaving a care situation denial by all concerned will be your major hazard and responsibility. Obviously everyone will need to know the practical arrangements, including the child, but you will be amazed at how many times these will need rehearsing. I suspect there is a 'law' – the longer the child has been in care, the more times you need to go through the arrangement for his discharge.

Going home after 'short-term' care

It is easy to say to parents: 'Just pop down to Mrs Jones and collect John any time that suits you and her' and ignore all the emotional factors of which you were aware at the time of admission to care. The same differences need to be considered now. A child will make the transition home more easily if a photograph of the principal carer can go with him, and possibly a new toy to which he has become attached in placement. He should be encouraged to leave something behind to return and visit.

If they have been doing their job in the most caring way possible, the foster mother or residential worker will have a lot of feelings about the child going. Remember that they will want to know how the child settles back home. They may also need preparation for some ambivalent behaviour on the part of the child when he comes on a return visit after going home (see Robertson (1969) film 'Sarah').

Preparation of the parents may be the hardest. They will not expect there to be changes in their child, and the confusion and anger these create in them will be hard for them to voice. They are likely to feel obligated to the authority and the carer, causing them to present passively or with hostility. Their sense of loss can be difficult for them to cope with. Their child may not welcome the return home, may be aggressive towards them, and regression is very common, including the return of enuresis. Some children refuse food on return home, and others need a great deal of extra cuddling. This does not mean they have been inappropriately fed or cuddled while in care, but is a response to the stress of change. Parents need to be prepared for this before it occurs, or your explanation may sound as if you are excusing poor care.

Often a child takes time to settle back home, longer than the parents imagine possible, for they want quickly to wipe out all the memories aroused by the child being away from them. Encourage the parent to take the child's cues about timing. You will need to help the parent with his feelings of guilt and his desire to overcompensate with sweets, or staying up late.

Where you have had a good relationship with the child while he was in care, try to prepare the parents to allow you to continue to see the child on his own once he has gone home. He will need to share with you common memories that may not be comfortable for him to bring to his parents, or may feel to him like betrayal of them. You can act as the bridge for these memories to be brought into the home situation. Parents may try to cast you into an 'inspector' with these visits to the child on his own, so aim to make them activity-centred, popping out to the park, or sharing for a few minutes in his bedroom and bringing out something to share with the parents afterwards.

Going home after 'long-term' care

Going out of care after a long spell of institutional living is a major trauma to any child. Parents who have been visiting him, or having him home on a 'treat' basis, now have the role of discipline-giver. A stepparent may have entered the domestic scene, changing all the roles and relationships at home. All these need discussion and rehearsal with the child. Home is likely to be smaller than the children's home, it may not be as warm, food may be culturally and quantitatively different, and money, clothing, furniture and social activities may be less easily available. (Poverty has been shown to be a major factor contributing to the numbers of children coming into care.)

Parents do not have off-duty times. Children used to demanding a great deal of adult attention may find the rivalries and limited resources of their parents difficult to tolerate, and need preparation for how to handle this. Residential staff can look at the implications of this with the attention-seeking youngster.

Schooling needs planning. The school near home may be of a different ethnic mix, with different academic expectations. Close liaison between the two schools needs to be set up, usually by the fieldworker, and this will need following up after the child is discharged from care. The adjustment to the loss of school friends, the stigma/status problem of being in care, and now wondering who you are, is a problem the child will find hard to grasp until he is experiencing it in his first term in the new school near home.

Timing is often adjusted to the adult's concepts rather than the child's. It is important to involve the child in thinking about when would be the easiest time to move, not just the great urge to get home. Help the child and the parents to think whether 'discharge day' is to be special or to be glossed over in a pattern of visits. Talk with the child about the implications of each to himself and to his parents. School holidays, sharing in an establishment holiday, having a holiday when none of the rest of the family is having one, may all form part of your considerations. The school year, birthdays, Christmas, may all influence the choice of the appropriate time for an older child to return home.

In work with the parents, many of the same considerations will apply as mentioned under 'short term'. There is likely to be a 'honeymoon' of good behaviour, followed by a period of acute testing to see if the parents will reject the child. The 'honeymoon' may last for up to two years, depending on how insecure the child feels in the home situation, and then when the challenge comes, the parents will not necessarily connect the change in behaviour with the 'in care' period at all. It is your task to prepare them for this possibility, even though you may be long out of the picture by the time the testing comes. More commonly, the difficult behaviour comes within a few weeks of discharge from care. It may include stealing at home or from local shops, regression, inordinate demands for material proof of security, night disturbance, school refusal, and the need for limits to be clearly set. Parents often find it difficult to share this with you unless you have prepared them for it beforehand, for they feel they are failing. Give them the opportunity to talk about tiredness, their inability to love the child all the time, their fears of disciplining him, that his being home 'won't work'. Help them to share with you the strains imposed on their marital relationship and the difficulties they are experiencing, while encouraging them to find their own solutions and reinforcing the strengths that exist in the relationship with the child. It may be necessary to help the parent organise shared activities with the child, in order to lessen the tension that builds up around the discipline issues.

The loss of shared activities is a major difficulty for many children going from communal living to a more isolated situation at home. Part of the preparation for discharge should be the encouragement of both child and parent to find some suitable local activities the child can enjoy while home for weekends and visits. Liaison with youth organisations may be a crucial tool in the adjustment to being at home, offering both parent and child the 'space' to be apart from each other.

Medical care and dentistry may need timing as part of the overall discharge plan. If the child is involved in church then this, too, needs some consideration. If he should be moving from one authority's area to another then some liaison work would be involved in ensuring that supervision is established in the new area, if you are not allowed to undertake this yourself. It is good practice, where possible physically, for the discharging authority to work with the family until the child is fully settled at home, simply notifying the local authority of the work being undertaken in its area.

If the child has been in care more than six months, aim to give him a written account of his time in care. I have chosen that time as a convenience. It would be good practice for every child to have such an account, but I recognise the pressures that push this to the back of the priorities. Include in this account the names of those who have cared for him, the addresses of where he has lived, the names and addresses of all schools he has been to, and the GP who was responsible for his health care. Don't forget to give him the reasons for each move while he was in care, even if the reasons are painful to him, or to you as the department's representative. Names of friends, teachers, clubs, pets etc. all help allow the memories to live on after discharge. Photographs help a lot, and it may be that one of your residential colleagues could help in preparing the written account, or taking the pictures, of the time in care as part of the task of preparing him for discharge.

The child's need for love and security, new experiences, praise and recognition, and responsibility (Kellmer Pringle 1974) need once more to be assessed. Each of these areas will necessitate some thought by you to consider how they are going to be met in the home situation and what facilities you may need to offer the family to ensure that the discharge is in the best interests of the child.

Many foster parents are excellent at undertaking the preparatory work needed for a child to make the transition home smoothly, but there may be some additional rivalry between them and the natural parent at this time. Ensuring the child has the skills to cope appropriately at home can be a rewarding way for the foster mother to cope with her own sense of loss, as well as being a practical help to the child.

Where a child has lived with a family for some years it will be vital that the connection is not severed suddenly and this may necessitate your battling with the local authority for fares for subsequent visits and payments to the foster parent under Section 1 of the Child Care Act 1980. Try to write an agreement about future visiting into your plans for discharge, preferably at a review where all the details of the discharge plan are finalised. This avoids some of the denial problems as all then receive a written confirmation of the plans.

Leaving care

Many of those leaving care are not going home. These are adolescents for whom care has, in some measure, failed, in that it has neither re-established them with their own families, nor provided them with substitute families. They have grown up in community care, often lacking in the ability to give them the capacity for independence that is needed. For youngsters like these there is a growing concern, and, in some areas, growth of appropriate provision for a continuing period after they are 18.

The Barnardo's 16 + scheme is one of the most comprehensive. This includes a hostel, a group of specialist workers, a sheltered housing scheme and a link to a housing co-operative. The youngsters are accepted into the hostel and prepared there for independent living; they are then supported in their first attempts at this in the sheltered housing scheme before gaining their own tenancy. Workers are in close contact with them to start with, and the contact is then lessened by agreement, as time progesses. The St Christopher's Fellowship in London has hostels from which boys can move on to more independent bed-sit living in a house where there are two wardens available to help sort out problems. Charles Burgess (1981) comments on the opportunity such schemes may offer to youngsters in care to move to appropriate areas for seeking work. He suggests that residential staff should seek to form links with small companies or services which offer informal induction or training schemes for youngsters, as a way of helping the youngsters in care to obtain suitable employment. He stresses that preparation for work includes accurate information on the best sources for the specific type of work being sought, how to approach it and the building of interview skills.

Lothian's 'Supported Accommodation' brings together many of the ideas and problems of this concept of after-care. Kay Carmichael, in her article in that publication, says 'the most important goal is for the person being helped to be given every opportunity to manage his own life, but this can only be done if the helpers believe that they have the capacity to do this ... if the helpers' attitudes are pessimistic and paternalistic, little growth will take place'. Their overall conclusion is that councils should have a range of provision available for all their vulnerable clients, who need supported accommodation. Linked to the accommodation there should be a central base where self-help support groups, volunteers, social workers, leisure activities and skills learning would be available according to need.

Leaving care requires special preparation in practical areas. Stan Godek's (1976) survey of youngsters leaving a particular Scottish provision outlines problems that need particular attention. Budgeting presents major difficulties for youngsters who have had no experience of the cost of rents, fuel and food. Looking after themselves may need new skills of washing and ironing clothes, sewing and cooking which, for boys, may also mean a re-think about their stereotype or class norms, not that they have to find a girl to do it all for them! Relating to their peers when they are not living in a ready-made group can be a major difficulty. They will have lost their companions and may fall into delinquency as a way of being involved with their peers to compensate for that loss. For girls there is the danger of becoming sexually 'easy' as a substitute for relating. There is often a lack of real understanding and knowledge about sexuality despite all the bravado. Contraception may be known about but not understood or accepted emotionally.

Work-related problems are particularly difficult for the youngster living alone after a long period of institutional care. He has little idea of how to negotiate time off to deal with his accommodation problems and his attitude to his boss and colleagues may be quite inappropriate, based on the easy interaction of the residential care team. There is the constant conflict of the desire to do things for himself and yet to have some dependency.

'We have to ensure that there is a sense of continuity and allow them to rebel. In this way we will enable them to rid themselves of dependence and institute self confidence' (Lenhoff 1968). This, then, is the role of the keyworker for the adolescent leaving care: to allow the rebellion, to continue to support and advise when the youngster may be rejecting, rude and appearing to want to be rid of you. A difficult task when the law says that at 18 the youngster has the right to choose to have no further contact, and you may be in the middle of that rebellion! Obviously we should be aiming at starting the process of preparation for leaving care at least before school leaving at 16. The close co-operation of the field and residential social worker during this period is probably the most crucial factor. Where there has been a close relationship with the residential worker the need for this to be loosened and transferred to the fieldworker will echo all the fears of loss that the young person is experiencing in leaving the establishment. At the end of the chapter I have included a check-list for a leaving plan, which you could use to identify who is going to undertake the different elements of the essential task.

In 1980 the Church of England Children's Society produced a handbook to give to children leaving their care called *Out of care – what now*. Local authorities need to look at the need for a similar book for all those leaving long-term care. Barnardo's comment that: 'Our after care work has no age limit . . . our young people may turn to us for help and advice in matrimonial difficulties or regarding old age pensions . . . a large number keep in touch with us . . . to let us know of their happiness and they enjoy our pleasure in this knowledge.' I can echo this as I have found delight in hearing from young people in their twenties whom I first knew as young children in care, but no child should have to rely on one person remaining in the job for that after-care to be available. We should be aiming at each young person being linked to a family who can offer continuity. This may not be full fostering, but a befriending can for many continue into adult life, and bridge the gap between care and out of care, in the way that in Cambridge-shire it bridges the gap between Intermediate Treatment and the scheme having finished (Green 1979).

Drawing it all together then, a young person should leave care with emotional preparation for coping alone, understanding of his rights to further help and where it may be available, and the ability to manage his physical well-being reasonably. Ideally he should have the right to some housing that offers him the opportunity to find employment, and knowledge of where leisure and further education is available. He should be in contact with supportive adults, to whom he can turn when faced with a crisis with which he feels unable to cope. He should know and understand about his own past and have a written account of his time in care, prepared either by himself or his social worker, and giving him the factual information he may need in adult life about his parents and his own past, including all relevant medical histories. In many authorities work with the 17-year-olds is regarded as minimal and often is only crisis-related. I would urge you to reverse this trend and regard the last eighteen months in care as offering the opportunity for preparation for adult life.

After care

The permissive powers to help those discharged from care by advising, befriending, visiting, supporting financially while in training, or in making available suitable accommodation for them to be in employment is one that is grossly underused by local authorities for those children who have been in their long-term care. Financial cuts have affected this area of concern as with many others. It is necessary to see help given to the 18-to-21-year-olds as investment for the future. Stability in employment, success in training achieved now, may be preventing the next generation from requiring assistance under the preventive powers of Section 1. Social workers are all aware of the second- and third-generation families in care and the opportunity to work with youngsters after their formal discharge from care should be seen as just as critical as that preventive work under Section 1. How many young people enter unsuitable liaisons during their late teens and early twenties, in order to find some support, some sense of security? Those who have been long term in care are particularly vulnerable and we should be offering them some real alternatives. Housing co-operatives and supported living schemes go some way to meet this need, but the first essential is that the social worker responsible at the time of discharge make it clear to the young person that he still has the right to call on the department for assistance. Like parents, local authorities who have undertaken the parental role towards the children in their care should not just disappear at the magic age of 18! While endless dependency is not to be encouraged, a realistic balance between the need for help and advice and the independence of the youngster concerned should be worked out to reflect the best interests of the individual concerned. We recognise that people mature at a different rate and different ages, and this should be reflected in our handling of the child's discharge from care and the after-care arrangements made.

Check-list 9 – *The legal implications of a child's age when he goes out of care*

Age 15: If sent to Borstal, then a care order is automatically cancelled.

Age 16+: Discharge from Section 2, Child Care Act 1980, care leaves a duty on a local authority to advise and befriend, unless it is satisfied that the welfare of the young person does not require it. The local authority in whose care the young person has been has a duty to notify any other local authority into whose area the young person may move, of that same duty, until he is 18. (Child Care Act 1980, Section 28).

Can get married with the consent of one parent, guardian or court. If in care, Section 2, this would constitute a discharge from care. If the child is the subject of a care order and marries with the consent of the parent rather than the authority then this does not invalidate the marriage, and the care order would automaticaly be discharged by the court on its being informed of the marriage.

Age 17+: Discharge from Section 2 care gives a permissive power to the local authority if requested by the young person to advise, befriend and in exceptional circumstances, help financially, until the young person is 21 (Child Care Act 1980, Section 29).

If left care, no matter what kind, after compulsory school leaving age, while he is under 21 the local authority *may* make contributions to accommodation, maintenance, education or training expenses. If finance is the only reason for a young person to stay in care after 17 he could be discharged and still receive financial help.

Age 18: Section 2 care ends. Care order made before sixteenth birthday or in court other than Juvenile Court ends. Can ask any local authority to visit, advise or befriend him, or to help him financially in exceptional circumstances.

Age 19: Care order made in Juvenile Court when he is 16 ends.

Age 21: Advise and befriend opportunities end, but any contributions or grants to maintenance for training continue until completion of the course, even if the course was interrupted by circumstances, provided it is resumed as soon as possible.

Check-list 10 – *Discharge from care*

Child in care short term (eight weeks or less)

1. Have I talked with the child and encouraged foster parents/residential social workers to do so about differences at home of food, bedtime, clothing, play space and toys, school or nursery, sharing, packing and taking things... leaving something for a subsequent visit if that is possible?

2. Have I prepared the parents for the child's: (a) lack of welcome, aggression, possible enuresis, punishment for desertion, refusal of food; (b) need to regress; (c) need for extra food, extra physical handling, time to settle back into the home?

3. Have I encouraged parents to share their: (a) guilt that the child has been in care; (b) feelings of inadequacy; (c) tendency to overcompensate now that their child is home; (d) anger/hostility/frustration (if any) with the foster parents and establishment?

4. Have I arranged when and how I'll let the carers know how the child has settled at home?

5. Have I fixed a return visit and prepared all concerned for the mixed feelings – parent's rivalry, child's confusion, wanting to and yet fearing the visit?

6. Have I arranged with parents and child to see child alone after he is home, explaining purpose, where appropriate (child's loss, guilt at feeling loss, memories parent has not had, anger with parent)?

Child in care long term

1. Have I prepared the *child* for: (a) change in parental role – from person who gives weekend treats to disciplinarian; (b) change in parental situation, e.g. new stepfather's role; (c) home – living with different standards of room size, etc.; (d) rivalries (new baby, step-siblings); (e) schooling differences – type, size of class, ethnic mix, academic expectations; (f) loss of peers – encouraging written contact where possible; (g) change in status – from being 'in a home' to being with parents – and explaining that comfortably?

2. Have I prepared the *parents* for: (a) behaviour problems, specifying what kinds they can expect; (b) setting boundaries, discussing with them what demands and expectations there have been in care and working out how to bridge differences between care and home; (c) responsibility for child in the community – links with school/Job Centre/college, medical care, social activities – clubs, organisations, facilities; (d) social worker's role after discharge?

3. Have I made sure everyone, including child, is clear about discharge plan (confirmed in writing) – visits, dates, holidays, where and with whom,

transport, whether or not discharge day is 'special' or glossed into a pattern of visits with a steady transfer of belongings?

4. Have I sorted out finances – increases in child benefit, family income supplement, supplementary benefit?

5. Have I clarified practical issues – e.g. school uniform changes, extra bed needed, enuresis requiring additional bedding and incontinent laundry assistance?

After discharge

1. Visits should continue until child is settled; no one can determine how long this is but child; remember child's need to deny previous life when assessing need to continue visiting.

2. Parents may need opportunity to talk about: (a) tiredness; (b) failure in self; (c) inability to love the child all the time; (d) disappointment/frustration; (e) financial nightmare; (f) the challenge to their marital *status quo*.

Check-list 11 – *An adolescent leaving care*

Staff discussion about resident leaving

Who does the leaver want to be on duty on last day? Can rotas be altered to accommodate? Who will escort to new living situation? Has leaver been consulted about the role of the residential worker? The social worker? Who will keep contact during first four weeks? Next three months? Subsequently? Are leavers' preferences about this known?

Exercise to focus on strengths and weaknesses in leaver to help in plan on p. 109.

Each member of staff completes the following two sentences with regard to the leaver:

I'll miss . . . most because . . .

I'll be glad when . . . has left because . . .

The group then discusses the difficulties in relationship thus revealed, and considers the ways in which the strengths can be underlined and enhanced.

Area to be covered with the leaver	*Initials of person responsible*	*Date planned*	*Date done*
Work experience and job counselling, finding out about training.			
Finding jobs, keeping them, handling problems at work.			
Telling about being in care.			
Claiming benefit.			
Budgeting, saving and banking, handling debts, HP.			
Medical cards and how to register with a GP.			
Housekeeping skills; cooking, cleaning, personal hygiene.			
Finding somewhere to live; tenancy problems; considerate behaviour; managing litter, repairs, etc.			
How to find leisure activities, community resources and use of time alone.			
Photographs of group and knowledge of how to contact them.			
Discussion group with other residents and the leaver about his departure.			
Discussion (and role play sessions) on:			
(a) solving family problems, practical and personal;			
(b) dealing with violence in oneself and others;			
(c) handling drinking/drug abuse problems;			
(d) interacting with others in society – opposite sex, officials, police, etc.;			
(e) finding information, making decisions, making plans.			

Exercise on discharge from short-term care

The James family live in two rented furnished rooms and kitchen, on the first floor sharing bathroom and W.C. with a very elderly woman downstairs. Two and a half months ago, Danny (aged 8) and Helen (aged 10) were received into care when their mother, Mrs James, went into hospital for a hysterectomy. The children expected to be in care for three weeks. Mr James is a heavy drinker, sometimes violent when drunk, and works shifts including nights. He has a motor bike, which his wife will not go on. He rarely takes care of the children. Mrs James and the social worker, who had only met the family regarding this reception into care, felt he was unable to look after the children. No 'home carer' or foster home was available. Mrs James is an only child and her elderly mother in Liverpool was not able to have the children or come to London. Relationships with Mr James's family are poor and there are no friends able to have the children.

Mrs James contracted a virus infection after the operation and was not discharged from hospital for six weeks. She has visited the children twice since her discharge three and a half weeks ago. Mrs James has been seen by the social worker six times in the nine and a half weeks the children have been in care. The children were taken to see her in hospital twice by the social worker, who formed a good relationship with them during the outings.

Helen and Danny are placed in Hollybush – a local authority children's home for twenty children; it is an hour's bus ride and a ten-minute walk from their home. It is run in two groups – Helen has been in one and her 'special worker' is Peter; Danny, in the other group, has Sonia as his 'special'. Peter is on duty today; when Mrs James visited neither Peter nor Sonia was on duty.

Mr James has visited the children several times a week and he has a good relationship with Peter, but has only seen the social worker once while the children have been in care. All the workers agree that the children's relationship with their father has improved while they have been in care.

Today Danny and Helen are being collected by their parents.

Tasks

1. Roles of Mr James, Mrs James, Danny, Helen, Peter and the fieldworker are allocated. They then form a tableau which demonstrates by their physical proximity or distance the emotions of each character at the point of discharge. Hands and arms, angle of head or body or height in relation to others, should all show each character's feelings. When all six are satisfied then the group 'freeze' – i.e. keep completely still for two minutes. During that time each thinks solely of their characters' feelings at the moment the children are being handed back to their parents. Each should notice what they feel about each of the others. After two minutes, break, and each should write down their feelings before the group shares.

2. What transport arrangements would be needed? What would different transport arrangements mean to the people involved in the discharge?

3. What preparation would you have done before discharge? What work do you expect to be needed after discharge?

Bibliography

ABAFA 1976, *Planning for children in long term care*, Association of British Adoption and Fostering Agencies

ABAFA 1977, *Working with children who are joining new families*, Association of British Adoption and Fostering Agencies

Ackerman, N. 1958, *The psycho dynamics of family life*, New York, Basic Books

Adams, R., Allard, S., Baldwin, J. and Thomas, J. (eds) 1981, *A measure of diversion? Case studies in intermediate treatment*, National Youth Bureau

Adcock, M. and White, R. 1977, *The assumption of parental rights and duties*, Association of British Adoption and Fostering Agencies

Alm, N. 1981, 'Dundee children's activity centres', Chapter 7 in R. Adams et al. (eds), *A measure of diversion? Case studies in intermediate treatment*, National Youth Bureau

Althea 1979, *My childminder*, Dinosaur Publications

Andrews, C. 1972, *Conflicts of identity in substitute care*, Annual Review of Residential Child Care Association

Association of the Directors of Social Services 1980, *Report of the 2nd survey of the extent and effects of cuts/savings in expenditure on the personal social services*, ADSS

Barker, P. (ed) 1973, *Care can prevent: child care or child psychiatry?* National Children's Home

Barritt, G. 1979, *Residential care: rehabilitating the child in care*, National Children's Homes Occasional Papers no. 2

Beedell, C. 1970, *Residential life with children*, Routledge & Kegan Paul – Library of Social Work

Berry, J. 1972a, *Social work with children*, Routledge & Kegan Paul – Library of Social Work

Berry, J. 1972b, 'The experience of reception into residential care' *British Journal of Social Work*, vol. 2, no. 4. pp. 423–34

Berry, J. 1977, *Daily experiences in residential life: a study of children and their care-givers*, Routledge & Kegan Paul – Library of Social Work

Bloom, C.V. 1969, *Children are our concern*, Dr Barnardo's

Bowlby, J. 1969, 1973, 1980, *Attachment and loss*, vols. 1, 2 and 3, Hogarth

Brill, K. 1962, *Children, not cases: social work for children and their families*, National Children's Home

Brown, B. 1978, 'Behavioural approaches to child care', *British Journal of Social Work* vol. 8, no. 3, autumn, pp. 313–26

Bruner, J. 1980, *Under 5 in Britain,* Grant McIntyre

Bryant, B., Harris, M. and Newton, D. 1980, *Children and minders*, Grant McIntyre

Burgess, C. 1981, *In care and into work*, Tavistock

Camden, London Borough of, Social Services Department 1980, *Straight answers – a handbook for young people in care*

Central Council for Education and Training in Social Work 1978, *Good enough parenting – report of a study group*, CCETSW

Central Policy Review Staff 1978, *Services for young children with working mothers*, HMSO

Challis, L. 1980, *The great under 5s' muddle*, University of Bath

Charnley, J. 1955, *The art of child placement*, University of Minnesota Press

Cheetham, J. 1972, *Social work with immigrants*, Routledge & Kegan Paul – Library of Social Work

Church of England Children's Society 1980, *Out of care – what now? A handbook for children leaving care*

Cooper, J. 1978, *Patterns of family placement – current issues in fostering and adoption*, National Children's Bureau

Coulter, A. 1981, *Who minds about the minders*, Low Pay Unit

Davies, B., Barton, A. and McMillan, I. 1972, *Variations in children's services among British urban authorities*, Papers on Social Administration no. 45

Department of Education and Science 1980, *Community homes with education. A survey of educational provision in 21 community homes with education on the premises (CHEs) in England and Wales 1978*, HMSO

Department of Health and Social Security Advisory Council on Child Care 1972, *Care and treatment in a planned environment – a report on the community homes project*, HMSO

Department of Health and Social Security Circular LAC (76) 15, *Children Act: programme for implementation in 1976/77*

Department of Health and Social Security 1976a, *Low cost day provision for under 5s*

Department of Health and Social Security 1976b, *Guide to fostering practice; a working party report* (Chairperson Janie Thomas), HMSO

Department of Health and Social Security Social Work Service Group 1978, *IT in action* (film), produced by Wessex Film and Video Productions (available from Social Work Service Development Group, DHSS, Elephant and Castle, London SE1

Department of Health and Social Security 1982a, *Children in care in England and Wales March 1980*

Department of Health and Social Security 1982b, *The study of the boarding out of children*, HMSO

Dockar Drysdale, B. 1973, *Consultation in child care – papers on residential work*, Longman

Durham County Council Social Services Department 1979, *Guide for children in care*

Eikenberry, D. 1969, 'A story for Mary', in E. Holgate (ed) 1972, *Communicating with children* Longman

Equal Opportunities Commission 1978, *I want to work but what about the kids* (day care for young children and opportunities for working parents), Equal Opportunities Commission

Ferri, E. and Niblett, R. 1977, *Diasdvantaged families and playgroups*, NFER

Foot, H., Chapman, A. and Smith, J. 1980, *Friendship and social relations in children,* Wiley

Gardiner, S. and Riddle, S. (eds) 1975, *A-Z of fostering for Camden,* London Borough of Camden Social Services Department

Godek, S. 1976, *Leaving care – Barnardo social work papers No. 2,* Dr Barnardo's

Goldstein, J., Freud, A and Solnit, A. 1973, *Beyond the best interests of the child,* Free Press

Goldstein, J., Freud, A. and Solnit, A. 1980, *Before the best interests of the child,* Burnett Books

Green, D. 1979, *Intermediate treatment befriending scheme,* Cambs Social Services

Hallett, C. and Stevenson, O. 1980, *Child abuse: aspects of inter-professional co-operation,* George Allen & Unwin

Hazel, N. 1981, *A bridge to independence – The Kent family placement project,* Blackwell

Heywood, J. 1978, 3rd ed, *Children in care,* Routledge & Kegan Paul

Heywood, J. and Allen, B. 1971, *Financial help in social work? A study of preventive work with families under the Children and Young Persons Act 1963,* Manchester University Press

Hill, M. and Laing, P. 1979, *Social work and money,* George Allen & Unwin

Hoggett, B. 1977, *Parents and children,* Sweet & Maxwell

Hoghui, M. 1980, *Assessing problem children: issues and practice,* Burnett Books/Deutsch

Holgate, E. (ed) 1972, *Communicating with children,* Longman

Holman, R. 1973, *Trading in children: a study of private fostering,* Routledge & Kegan Paul

Holman, R. 1976, *Inequality in child care,* Child Poverty Action Group

Home Office 1968, *Children in trouble,* Cmnd 3601, HMSO

Hudson, J. 1980, 'When is prevention better than care?' *Social Work Today,* vol. 11, no. 46, 5 August

Hughes, M. *et al.* 1980, *Nurseries now: a fair deal for parents and children,* Penguin Books

Jackson, B. and S. 1979, *Childminder,* Routledge & Kegan Paul

Jackson, S. 1979, *Out of school – how to set up after school and holiday schemes for children of working parents,* Bristol Association for Neighbourhood Day care (BAND) and the UK Association for the International Year of the Child

Jordan, W. 1972, *The social worker in family situations,* Routledge & Kegan Paul – Library of Social Work

Kahan, B. 1979, *Growing up in care,* Blackwell

Kendon, O. 1979, *'Because they asked', being the story of Olive Kendon and why and how she founded the Children's House Society,* The Children's House Society

Kerslake, A. and Jones, R. 1979, *Intermediate treatment and social work,* 1979 Community Care Practice Handbooks, Heinemann Educational Books

Knight, B. *et al.* 1979, *1979 Family groups in the community,* London Voluntary Service Council

Lasson, I. 1978, *Where's my mum?* Pepar

Lawson, A. 1980, 'Taking the decision to remove the child from the family', *Journal of Social Welfare Law*, May

Leach, P. 1979, *Who cares? A new deal for mothers and their small children*, Penguin Books

Leeding, A. 1978, 4th edn, *Child care manual for social workers*, Butterworths

Lenhoff, F. G. 1968, *Learning to live*, Shotton Hall Publications

Lothian Regional Council Department of Social Work 1975, *Planning for children in care*, Interim report of a working party on the implication of the Children Act 1975

Lothian Regional Council Department of Social Work, ND, *Final report of a departmental working party on some of the implications of the Children Act 1975*

Lothian VORAG 1976, *Supported accommodation: issues, ideas and practice*, Lothian Regional Department of Social Work

Mayall, B. and Petrie, P. 1977, *Minder, mother and child*, University of London Institute of Education

Millham, S. *et al.* 1980, *Give and take – a study of CSV's project for young people in care*, Dartington Social Research Unit, Community Service Volunteers, 237 Pentonville Road, N1

Mulvey, T. 1976, 'After care who cares? A study of young people who have left care at the statutory age of 18', Unpublished thesis for Essex University, available at National Children's Bureau

Murray, A. and Porteous, B. 1981, 'Personal beliefs and the experience of problems – a study in adolescence, *British Journal of Social Work* vol. 11, no. 1, pp. 43–60

National Childminding Association 1979, *Report of the working party on the training of childminders*, National Childminding Association

National Childminding Association 1980, *Guide for childminders groups*, National Childminding Association

National Children's Bureau 1978, *Development guide 0–5 years*, National Children's Bureau

National Foster Care Association, 1981, *Foster Care*, Francis House, Francis Street, London SW1Q 1DE

O'Brien, D. 1980, *From Residential to day assessment in Belfast*, Chapter V in R. Walton and D. Elliott (eds), *Residential reader*, Pergamon

Office of Population Censuses and Surveys 1982, *Social Trends*, no. 12

Orlin, M. 1977, 'Resolving conflicts in foster care', *Adoption and Fostering*, vol. 90

Packman, J. 1973, 'Incidence of need', quoted in J. Stroud (ed), *Services for children*, Pergamon

Packman, J. 1975, *The child's generation: child care policy from Curtis to Houghton*, Blackwell & Robertson

Page, Raissa, and Clark, G. A. 1977, *Who cares? Young people in care speak out*, National Children's Bureau

Paley, J. and Thorpe, D. 1974, *Children: handle with care*, National Youth Bureau

Parker, R. 1966, *Decision in child care*, George Allen & Unwin

Parker, R. 1971, *Planning for deprived children*, National Children's Homes

Parker, R. 1980, *Caring for separated children*, National Children's Bureau

Payne, C. and White, K. 1979, *Caring for deprived children*, International case studies of residential settings

Priestley, P. *et al.* 1978, *Social skills and personal problem solving – a handbook of methods*, Tavistock

Pringle, M. K. 1974, *The needs of children*, Hutchinson (paperback 1975)

Prosser, H. 1978, *Perspectives on foster care*, NFER

Ravenette, A. T. 1977, 'Psychological investigation of children and young people', in D. Bannister (ed), *Perspectives in personal construct theory*, Academic Press

Reinach, E. and Roberts, G. 1979, *Consequences*, Social Services Research and Intelligence Unit, Portsmouth Polytechnic

Richards, H. 1979, 'The wishes and needs of the child', in *Adoption and Fostering*, vol. 96

Richards, M. 1974, *The integration of a child into a social world*, Cambridge University Press

Robertson, J. 1969, *Sarah*, Tavistock Institute of Human Relations (film)

Rowe, J. and Lambert, L, 1973, *Children who wait – a study of children needing substitute families*, Association of British Adoption Agencies

Rutter, M. 1972, *Maternal deprivation reassessed*, Penguin Books

Rutter, M. 1975, *Helping troubled children*, Penguin Books

Schaffer, H. and Schaffer, E. 1968, *Child care and the family: a study of short term admission to care,* Occasional papers on administration no. 25, Bell

Scottish Council for Single Homeless and Scottish Association of Voluntary Child Care Organisations 1976, *After care – where? A report of the study day, 10 December*

Sheridan, M. 1975, 3rd edn, *Birth to five years*, Children's Developmental Progress from NFER

Simpson, R. 1978, *Day care for school age children*, Equal Opportunities Commission

Steer, G. and Wallis Myers, J. 1962, *After care*, Dr Barnardo's

Thoburn, J. 1980, *Captive clients – social work with families of children home on trial*, Routledge & Kegan Paul

Thorpe, D., Green, C. and Smith, D. 1980a, *Punishment and welfare: case studies of the workings of the 1969 Children and Young Persons Act*, Occasional papers in Social Administration no. 4, Centre of Youth, Crime and Community, Dept of Social Administration, University of Lancaster

Thorpe, D., Smith, D, Green, C. J. and Paley, J. H. 1980b, *Out of care: the community support of juvenile offenders* George Allen & Unwin (for the Centre of Youth, Crime and Community, Dept of Social Administration, University of Lancaster/.

Timms, N. 1969, *Casework in the child care service*, Butterworth

Tizard, B. 1977, *Adoption: a second chance*, Open Books

Tizard, J. 1978, 'Nursery needs and choices', chapter 6 in J. Bruner and A. Garton (eds), *Human growth and development,* Clarendon Press

Tizard, J., Moss, P. and Perry, J. 1976, *All our children – pre-school services in a changing society*, Temple Smith

Tizard, J., Sinclair, I. and Clarke, R. (eds) 1975, *Varieties of residential experience*, Routledge & Kegan Paul

Tod, R. (ed) 1971, *Social work in foster care: collected papers*, Longman

Tod, R. (ed) 1972, *Disturbed children*, Longman

Varma, V. (ed) 1973, *Stresses in children*, University of London

Ward, L. 1981, 'Entry into care – an admission of failure?' *Social Work Today*, vol. 12, no. 26, 3 March

Willans, A. 1977, *Breakaway – family conflict and the teenage girl*, Maurice Temple Smith

Willmott, P. and Mayne, S. 1980, 'The gingerbread boys and girls', *Community Care*, no. 311, 17 April, pp. 14–16

Winnicott, C. 1964, *Child care and social work: a collection of papers written between 1954–1963*, Codicote Press

Winnicott, D. 1965, *The maturation process and the facilitating environment*, Hogarth Press

Wolff, S. 1973, *Children under stress*, Penguin Books

Younghusband, E. 1965, *Social work with families: readings in social work*, vol. 1 George Allen & Unwin

Index